What

Theology?

DATE DUE			

Zaccheus Studies: Theology
Monika Hellwig, Editor

What Is
Theology?

by
J.J. Mueller, S.J.

A Michael Glazier Book
THE LITURGICAL PRESS
Collegeville, Minnesota

About the Author

J.J. Mueller, S.J., is an Associate Professor of Theology at St. Louis University. He is a former director of the Religious Studies graduate program at Gonzaga University, Spokane, Washington and is the author of *Faith and Appreciative Awareness* and *What Are They Saying About Theological Method?* He is also a frequent contributor to scholarly journals in the theological field.

A Michael Glazier Book published by The Liturgical Press

Cover design by Maureen Daney; typography by Edith Warren

TABLE OF CONTENTS

Editor's Note on Zacchaeus Studies

This series of short texts in doctrinal subjects is designed to offer introductory volumes accessible to any educated reader. Dealing with the central topics of Christian faith, the authors have set out to explain the theological interpretation of these topics in a Catholic context without assuming a professional theological training on the part of the reader.

We who have worked on the series hope that these books will serve well in college theology classes where they can be used either as a series or as individual introductory presentations leading to a deeper exploration of a particular topic. We also hope that these books will be widely used and useful in adult study circles, continuing education and RENEW programs, and will be picked up by casual browsers in bookstores. We want to serve the needs of any who are trying to understand more thoroughly the meaning of the Catholic faith and its relevance to the changing circumstances of our times.

Each author has endeavored to present the biblical foundation, the traditional development, the official church position and the contemporary theological discussion of the doctrine or topic in hand. Controversial questions are discussed within the context of the established teaching and the accepted theological interpretation.

We undertook the series in response to increasing interest among educated Catholics in issues arising in the contemporary church, doctrines that raise new questions in a contemporary setting, and teachings that now call for wider and deeper appreciation. To such people we offer these volumes, hoping that reading them may be a satisfying and heartening experience.

Monika K. Hellwig
Series Editor

Preface

One might expect a book entitled *What is Theology?* to be an abstract treatise about stuffy definitions, timeworn ideas, and academic exercises. But that is not my experience of theology. Theology is about people! It expresses our struggles with pain, loneliness, fear, confusion, and anxiety, as well as our exuberance in moments of joy, fellowship, goodness, belongingness, and love. It is from these experiences that theology receives its dynamism. What theology seeks to understand is the passionate love between God and humanity. "Passionate" is hardly the adjective one would expect, given its current connotation. But "passion" comes from the Greek word "to suffer," and actually refers to an enduring love that perseveres by commitment through all obstacles. It is faithful love that continues even if one person walks away from it. It expresses a relationship that takes many twists and turns—but always stays within the greater context of enduring love.

The greatest expression of this enduring love between God and humanity is Jesus. At the end of Jesus' life came his passion and death. Here "passion" describes his suffering love, and by extension, the faithful love God gives us even when we do not deserve it. Even when the disciples walked away, the suffering love of Jesus did not leave them. As Christians, we believe that Jesus revealed a passionate God, one who suffers and cares for us and who chooses to be involved in a love relationship with us. We are loved and we make a difference, to God and to one another.

Theology expresses this passion of God, our response, and the story that emerges. God's passionate love calls forth the same response from us. And that is where theology begins.

This book, then, is about passion. It will treat abstract ideas, concepts, constructs, models, and relationships, but with the awareness that they only touch the tip of the iceberg, and only love can melt the whole. When we begin to explore, we must remember that theology is about people, loved by a passionate God. This is its history; its content; its purpose.

This book is the first in the Zacchaeus doctrinal series. It opens up topics which will be treated later in more detail. What matters now is the context for doing theology. The way one approaches theology influences how one perceives and uses the information received. This volume is important for those just entering the field of theology. It is also an important summary for those who have already studied theology in its many parts. The purpose of this study is to draw a big picture, showing the general context of all theological endeavor. It is, necessarily, written from one theologian's perspective. But it is essentially a question, not a statement of opinion. How will you, the reader, approach theology? How will you use theological training?

Whether I am successful in presenting the totality of theology- the passion and not just our intellectual understanding of it— remains for you to judge. I draw upon the passion of many other theologians—Rahner, Lonergan, Tracy, Meland, Schillebeeckx, Gutierrez, et. al.—and many students who have taught me about theology. But the failures in this book are mine, not theirs.[1]

I especially wish to thank my students over the years, the faculties of Gonzaga University (Spokane, Washington) and St. Louis University (St. Louis, Missouri), my theological colleagues, the John Courtney Murray Group in American philosophal theology, the Jesuit community, and many friends and family members. In different ways, they have all expressed this passionate love from which my theology derives, the love this book seeks to show.

---

[1]Throughout the book I struggled to find an alternative to the masculine pronoun in referring to God. The present structure of the language offered me few options. In the interest of clarity, I used the masculine pronoun, realizing all the while it was inadequate. For, as Genesis 1:27 tells us, "God created man in his image; in the divine image he created him; male and female he created them."

Introduction

What is theology? Etymologically, the word means "talk about God." But not everything we say about God can be considered theology. In the eleventh century, Anselm defined theology as "faith seeking understanding." This definition captures the enterprise of theology: it begins with the human experience of faith, and seeks to make it explicit by understanding all it signifies, means and implies. But the definition falls short of completion. Theology does not float by itself like a balloon on the end of a string. Faith seeks understanding so that understanding can contribute to faith. We do not theologize because we are theologians but because we are human. We begin with human experience, make a full circle, and return enriched, but still human.

Because theology springs from the faith of people, theology belongs to people of faith. It is a social act. No one person can claim the totality of theology any more than one person can claim the totality of human experience. Thus, theology has a series of concentric social circles to which it is responsible. First, it is responsible to the faith of the individual; second, it is responsible to the faith community and the tradition it represents; third, it is responsible to all of humanity, even those who do not believe. Theology can claim no exemption from human responsibility; it is part of humankind's search for God and our humanity in God. The fundamental presupposition in Christian theology is that God loves everyone and extends salvation to everyone. Any truth revealed is not for private use; it is given to us all. Because faith is a social act made by individuals, theology must be also. Therefore theology should never be narrow-minded, stingy, possessive, or exclusive; but should be broad-minded, generous, open, and inclusive.

The practitioner of theology is certainly the theologian. However, the theologian can never claim exclusive rights to the doing of theology. Just as a surgeon practices medicine when she operates on the torn ligaments in a patient's knee, so too does a mother practice medicine when she pours antiseptic over her son's scraped knee. Just as a theologian practices theology when he studies the meaning of the resurrection in scripture, so too does a plumber when he talks about death with a friend who is dying. Theology is a process of faith seeking understanding that begins in every human person, then finds some of its understandings formulated into specified areas. Both the doctor (an M.D.) and the theologian (a Ph.D.) go beyond the ordinary practice open to most people. They specialize in knowing how and why these treatments work, and they look constantly for new possibilities. The specialists may not be the ones who pour the antiseptic or sit with the dying friend, but they are the ones who know when and why to suggest these "treatments."

The comparison between medicine and theology is an apt one. Both seek the health of the individual and the community. Medicine's domain is physiological; theology's domain is spiritual. But both seek salvation. The word "salvation" comes from the Latin "to save" or "to be safe," "to have well-being." And "well-being" means "being well" on all levels of human living. Neither medicine nor theology can afford to limit their domain to one area; they must include every dimension of being well. The psychological, emotional, and spiritual dimensions of a person are affected by biological health or sickness. So too are the biological, emotional, and psychological dimensions affected by spiritual health or sickness. Each specialty addresses well-being in a different domain but recognizes the inter-connectedness and integrity of the one human person.

As our understandings are gathered, ordered, systematized, and explained, recognizable areas of theology emerge. It is important to remember that theology did not float down ready-made from heaven; it is a product of human understanding. Theology is neither faith nor a substitute for it. Theology is a fallible enterprise that continues to relate the eternal truths of faith to the human experience, which is always contemporary. Thus theology is time-bound, historical, reformable and fallible.

Its formulations disclose the relationship of God to us, but they never exhaust the meaning of that relationship.

Imagine a wide river like the Mississippi or any other large river. The current runs faster and deeper in the mainstream, while the banks tug at the sides and slow it down. As the water fights with the dirt bank about the shifting territory, sometimes it swirls in circles. At other times it bounces against the bank and sends ripples back and forth across itself. Jostled, moving at different speeds, the river relentlessly continues downstream. It swings wide around a bend, narrows, then overflows into the fields, its shape changing with each change in terrain. The river also has moods: at times peaceful and calm, at other times ominous and raging. Through it all, rich deposits from upstream are being carried down to nourish the environment which supports life.

The water is faith. Theology is that river of water formed into a specific shape. The river begins in the collection of tributaries that feed the river. New tributaries enter all the time down the river's route. The word "tradition" in Latin means "to be carried." Every person's faith is carried down from the faith of those who have gone before. These persons, events, symbols, and writings form rich deposits within that great river. Because of the world's different people, cultures, and circumstances, many theologies mix together from the past to form one giant river of faith. Some of these theologies are mainstream: so many people found them correctly articulating the faith that they became central currents, racing headlong into the future and pushing other theologies to the sides. The attraction and staying power of Augustinian and Thomistic theologies certainly contribute to form this mainstream current. Theologies that respond to particular social and religious circumstances have either moved to the side or become deeply submerged in the flowing river, possibly to surface at a later time. Because theology flows down through time, through both favorable and unfavorable circumstances, it can either rage or peacefully flow. Above all, theology always moves down stream; although it remains identifiably theology, it continues to move and change in history.

What we consider clear and unassailable today will pass into the wider river of theology and perhaps not be as important in expressing faith tomorrow. Whether today's theology becomes mainstream tomorrow is not the point. Theology's task is to nourish faith with rich deposits. Tomorrow's nourishment will come from today's water. Like that river, theology will keep moving downstream so that it can continue to nourish life.

It might be noted that no riverbed can successfully contain all the water. The water of faith flows over fields and meadows, and draws fresh water from rains that come from heaven. Because faith connects us with God, it extends over the face of the earth like the rain, and only some of it collects in the river. But what does collect can be used; life can be continually drawn from it.

Doctrinal theology, to which this Zacchaeus series attends, expresses the teachings that have comprised the history of our faith. The topics that recur in our common experience and are represented in this enterprise are: God and related areas (trinity, unity, revelation, creation); Jesus and related areas (salvation, its history, its continuation, grace); ourselves and related areas (church, sacraments, other faiths). In addition to doctrinal theology, there are scriptural and moral theology. Different ways of distinguishing these areas are possible; there are many right answers. Today, there are several new theological frameworks, but they still include these three areas. Doctrine, scripture and morality remain the basic concerns of believers. Thus, we have teachings (doctrines) about what we believe in these areas. Although these teachings are ours and the formulations ours, we did not make up the content. God did that by loving us and relating to us. This assurance is solid, and we lean upon it with our lives.

How then shall we proceed? Most theology books adopt a logical order beginning with the existence of God as one and triune, then considering the incarnation of the Word in Jesus followed by the meaning of salvation, and finally discussing the church as the extension of this salvation history. I am proposing an entirely different approach. Instead of a logical model, I propose an experiential model based upon the sequence experience-reflection-experience. The reasons are clear. First, theology begins in human faith, so it begins in human anthropology. By itself, this is not new. Theologians since Vatican II have continually turned to human anthropology. Second, our faith experience finds its center in the normative event of Jesus who both interprets our experience and reveals God. Third, we will move from the human to Jesus and then to God. Only in Jesus does the revelation of the trinity come to light. Fourth, from Jesus and God our understanding of the importance of revelation in Jesus takes on meaning. We are constituted as disciples in the community called church, with all the relationships that implies. By proceeding this way, I hope to allow the reader to relive the history of theology from the inside out. It is not a series of external understandings but the best expression of the pursuit of understanding as we have experienced it in the past, and so we live it today.

While this is my model, its presentation has to take on a slightly different form. Our aim is to explain the content and context of theology. Therefore the book proceeds in four sections: (1) human anthropology as the framework for explaining the major concepts, or building blocks, which govern subsequent theologies (e.g. sin, salvation, faith). (2) The three central concepts that relate with human anthropology: Jesus, God, and Us. These three form a triad of relationships among themselves: theology cannot remove any one of them or the whole enterprise falls apart. (3) The forms we use to communicate theology, most specifically language and texts. (4) Finally, because the discussion of what is theology cannot be separated from the question of who is doing theology, a profile of a theologian. (Or what one can expect to happen when one undertakes the study of theology.) This profile will bring us full circle: as we began in human experience, so too will we end in the human experience of the theologian.

1

The Context of Theology

1. Theological Anthropology: Genesis

Karl Rahner correctly reflected that whatever we say about God says something about us; and whatever we say about ourselves says something about God. God and humanity are correlative terms. If either God or humanity did not exist, theology would be meaningless. It is no wonder that theology begins in the human experience of God. This understanding of the human person in relation to God is called theological anthropology. More and more often it is the starting point for reflection on doctrine. The approach theological anthropology takes is referred to, using spatial imagery, as movement "from the bottom up." (A "top down" approach to doctrine begins from the revelation of God, reasoning logically that, as most important, God should come first. But even the top down approach implies human experience.)

When speaking about humanity, about where and how human beings came into existence and what we are on earth for, Christian anthropology returns to the book of Genesis. This first book of the Bible speaks about the "beginnings" of human beings as related to God and to all subsequent history. It makes no pretense of being a statement of scientific fact (e.g. biological, geological, sociological) or a literal explanation of creation. It seeks to present the *deepest* truth of our existence. Myth, from the Greek, means a "story." The story of Adam and Eve is an origin myth which acts as the most powerful statement of truth about ourselves and God. Its truth is affirmed over and over again by every generation. Because mythic truth lies so deep within the human psyche, every nation, culture, and people has some type of origin myth.

Not only do origin myths speak of beginnings, they also describe endings. The endings are described in terms of purpose: how we are to be human. Thus they are not stories about the past so much as the present. When we dip into our memories and tell stories about the past, we are really telling something important about the present and the direction for the future. For example, when a presidential candidate in the United States campaigns, he tells stories about George Washington, 1776, Abraham Lincoln, the Civil War, etc., and he calls forth the identity of a people, fires their emotions, and presents the act of voting for him as a patriotic duty. The great stories of our country provide the context both for understanding ourselves and for taking action. Hence, we look forward by looking backward. We acknowledge the historical forces that carried us here and we look to unleash them in new ways for the future.

Origin myths are paradigms for understanding humanity and God. As "origins," they push the frontier of human knowing to its limit in order to explain who we are, where we come from, what our purpose is, and to whom we are connected. Because an origin myth deals with vague territory at the frontier of human knowing, the myth uses images and symbols to point to a reality that resists any final and definitive explanation. Like a yolk surrounded by its albumen, humanity is surrounded by a greater reality. Moreover, this reality is not a thing but a person called God. We are overtaken and grasped by what remains an unyielding mystery. The way the origin myth describes and orders our relation to this mystery becomes the way we communicate it to one another. Commonly accepted, it becomes a paradigm, i.e., the beginning of our considerations, on which others build. The origin myth of the book of Genesis is no exception. It forms the basic Christian anthropology for theology. True, new understandings of humanity continue to occur, but the origin remains the same. While new origin myths are possible, Adam and Eve remain the paradigm of human anthropology. Any understanding of theology must come to grips with this myth's contribution and continuing statement about humanity and God.

In Christian theology, the themes of the fall, sin, and salvation begin in the Genesis account and continue to this day. Because the event of Jesus is couched in these themes, any understanding of theology must return to them. Let us briefly return, then, to this origin myth and renew our understanding of human anthropology.

To begin with, and contrary to popular belief, the book of Genesis contains not one but two creation accounts. There is no attempt to reconcile them. Like blocks, they stand side by side. In the first account, which is the more recent of the two, creation takes place in seven days. Humanity, represented in Adam and Eve, is created on the sixth day as the culmination of all creation. The second and older account begins in the opposite way, placing the creation of Adam and Eve at the beginning to indicate the centrality of humanity to creation.

While the task of Scripture scholars is to work on the particular sources and exegesis of these two accounts, our concern is the theological meaning and implication of this origin myth for Christian anthropology. Because the story of Adam and Eve's creation, test, and disobedience are familiar to us, we can move to the distinctively theological implications.

First of all, Adam and Eve are created by God. This relationship of humanity to God cannot be overestimated. It sets forth the most fundamental truth of human living: we come from God and return to God. Second, Adam and Eve possess a familiarity with God which shows when they walk and talk with God face to face, as directly and freely as is humanly possible. Thomas Aquinas in the thirteenth century would continue this image in his use of the "beatific vision" ("blessed vision" of God face to face) as the goal of human life and the intimacy of heaven. Judaism said that no one could see the face of God and live, and even the great prophet Moses could not become so familiar with God. Moses was once allowed to see the back of God. Throughout the Judeo-Christian history, the analogy of seeing God has been consistently used to explain intimacy and familiarity with God. One need not trust, one can see for him or her self and deal with God directly.

Thus intimacy with God, and not the created world around them, is the human crown and glory, and Adam and Eve present this truth. Because they know their maker and deal with

God straightforwardly, peace and harmony flow. Their correct relationship with God is mirrored in every other relationship, including the abundance of nature's crops and benign domination of all animals.

Adam and Eve also know God's will for them: they are not to eat of the fruit of the tree of the knowledge of good and evil. While knowledge of God is their glory, freedom is humanity's chief characteristic. When Satan tempts them, they eat from the tree of the knowledge of good and evil. Evil enters into the world. The battle lines of history are drawn, with good on one side and evil on the other. Human freedom has altered the desired relationship by God: intimacy is lost, God is hidden, nature resists human control and all that the garden offered is now closed off. In short, a rupture of humanity's relationship with God has occurred. But the story has not ended. Its surprising conclusion is that God has not abandoned us. Salvation history begins. And by the same activities as Adam and Eve, namely trust and obedience, humanity struggles to return to that correct relationship with a gracious God.

As the great experiment failed, so will salvation succeed. But this is not clear until triumphantly the death and resurrection of Jesus overcomes sin once and for all. The forces of darkness seek to prevail with their ultimate threat of death but, because of Jesus, they will not succeed. Victory has come. In the meantime, throughout the Old Testament, restoration of the correct relationship between God and humanity comes through trust and obedience to God. Yet the tragic flaw of free will's ability to choose evil remains.

The Old Testament scriptures are a story woven around the themes of obedience and disobedience, trust and mistrust, freedom and slavery. Each is a variation of the same theme. Abraham, Isaac, Jacob, Joseph, Moses, David, and the prophets echo this theme in their stories. Even in the New Testament, especially in the Gospels, the obedience of Jesus to the Father clearly overcomes evil and is part and parcel of salvation. Paul understands Jesus as the "new adam" and the results of grace as the "new creation": intimacy is restored in the Holy Spirit and the correct relationship restored by an act of self-emptying on God's part. Hence obedient love is the manner of Jesus' life, and becomes our salvation as well. Whereas the garden was lost, the

Kingdom of God was given. Reflecting on the magnificence of such a gift, Augustine exclaimed and the Easter liturgy yearly proclaims what a happy fault that merited such a redeemer! It seems as though the solution exceeded the problem.

The presentation of Adam and Eve, however, does not stop with them—just like sin never stops with me but affects everyone around me. The second part of sin takes its effect in the Genesis account. How sorrowful this consequence is. Adam and Eve also are parents of humanity. They have two children: Cain and Abel. These brothers represent all the children of Adam and Eve even down to the present time. We know the tragic event of Cain killing Abel, but what we need to reflect on is why it happened and what it implies about our relationship to one another.

Cain and Abel can only be understood in light of the story of their parents' actions and the evil that resulted. Whereas Adam and Eve severed the relationship with God, perhaps we can call it their vertical relationship, Cain and Abel show that without God the relationship of brother to brother (or sister), the horizontal relationship, is also severed. Thus the human family falls apart in the ultimate human annihilation: brother murders brother. Because God is not in the picture, the correct relationship of brother to brother is ruptured. Mistrust and disobedience by humanity has resulted in disobedience and mistrust of brother to brother. In other words, correct relationship with one another flow from a correct relationship with God. The human tragedy of sin is not only alienation from God but also alienation from one another. War, violence, oppression, and injustice testify to the tragic consequences. The episode of the tower of Babel which follows the Cain and Abel account, whereby humanity is thrown into further separation by different languages, reinforces the deepening fraternal alienation resulting from sin.

Put schematically, the human community needs restoration of the vertical dimension of God and, at the same time, the horizontal dimension of brother and brother (sister). Jesus' message to love God above all and your neighbor as yourself sums up the correct relationship in both directions. God graciously offers us Jesus as the reconciliation of our relationship to the divine and to each other. Christology then becomes a central concern for all theology, a topic we will treat later.

In summary, no matter what origin myth one holds, the Genesis origin myth remains a paradigm in Christian theology. We hold that humanity is from God, that we belong to God and God to us, that we belong to one another as brother and sister under the same God, that we were created good but that we can go astray, that we depend on God to help us, to save us. Several theological terms spell out these various relationships and deserve further treatment: they are the subject of our next section.

2. Theological Building Blocks

The Genesis account of Adam and Eve not only serves to explain the origin of humanity but also introduces the basic concepts of the Christian religion. On closer examination we realize that every human person wrestles with the reality indicated by these concepts. Hence other religions such as Buddhism, Hinduism, and Islam share the same concerns. They refer to what is evil, what is good, and the goal of life. In the Judeo-Christian tradition these concepts are described in terms of sin, faith, and salvation. They form the most general framework for God-talk (theology). They are similar to the canvas whether as small as a match cover or as large as a wall, upon which an artist chooses to paint. The mythos of Adam and Eve paints reality in bold, broad brush strokes on a very large canvas, delineating only in a general way the meaning of these concepts.

In general, the Genesis account expresses the goal for humanity as "salvation," the meaning of evil as "sin," and good as "faith." In a real way, theology tries to render these ideas understandable in light of the Christian experience. Each of these concepts requires additional contributing concepts to explain, nuance, and complete their meaning, and bring to light the various relationships involved. To interrelate the whole as if systematizing these various relationships is the proper work of systematic or doctrinal theology. These additional concepts will be treated in later chapters. For now, let us begin with the three basic building blocks.

A. SIN

We are born into the middle of history. While the Genesis account explains our beginning, we now live in the middle of the story with many subsequent twists and turns: militarism, sexism, racism, and injustices of the twentieth century variety. Like Adam and Eve, the presence of evil rather than good jars and disturbs us. Let us begin with the concept of sin, what we do not want, in order to understand salvation, what we do want. We will first ask what the nature of sin is and then proceed to understand its implications for our lives today.

The etymology of the word sin is "to miss the mark." The word comes from ordinary experiences where the correctness of the world, its order, its proper relationships join together. For instance, one throws a rock at an oak tree; the aim, the throw, the distance, and the accuracy all come together as the rock hits the "mark," the tree. When one or more of the necessary conditions break down, the rock misses the mark. Since we are speaking about human persons and not rocks, the analogy refers to the harmony, correctness, and direction of life. Not to direct the aim of one's life toward God is to miss the mark of what it means to be human. It is to sin. Our happiness comes from our union with what God wants and has made us to be. As with Adam and Eve, if we are to become what God wants us to be, then freedom is implied. The choice to say yes or no in the direction of my life is the condition for sin. As the Genesis account so well describes, our mind and free choice are at once humanity's privilege and its burden. Both salvation and damnation rest upon our ability to make free choices.

As in the garden of Eden, life was meant to be harmonious and easy. We experience sin when life jars, conscience is forsaken, and evil is chosen. When a person lies, for instance, many bad effects tag along and the situation deteriorates. People cease to trust each other and, in general, human relationships break down. The story of Adam and Eve tells the sad story of the lie—by Satan who says they can be like God and then by Adam and Eve who stay away from God's familiar call. Their embarrassment at being naked prompts them to hide. Their punishment is a hard life of struggle and work, tilling the soil and bearing children with nature resisting their efforts.

From the beginning of creation, human persons have an intended purpose, otherwise to "miss the mark" would be meaningless. Genesis tells us our purpose: to relate to God. The specific implications of relating to God are not mentioned: seemingly an allowance for many types of relationships with God. Genesis, as all myth, writes in bold and broad strokes, leaving the details for us to fill in.

What Genesis does indicate is that obedience to God is at the heart of the relationship. Adam and Eve were disobedient, and only obedience by the human community can heal the damage. This obedience must be freely chosen. If persons fail to obey God, then they miss the mark and deviate from their intended purpose. Notice that this purpose includes all human persons. No one is excluded. Hence salvation, or the goal of humanity, belongs to all men and women without exception, and all are called to God. There are many paths but they all demand obedience.

Each choice we make contributes to a way of life. As Adam and Eve dramatically show, some free choices are major life choices while others are small. Sin refers both to the individual act and to the way of life it shapes. Often people focus only on the individual act as sin and forget the larger context, the life choice.

For example, telling a lie may be an example of a good person telling an expedient untruth to get out of an embarrassing situation. Or, telling a lie may be an example of a person entering into a deceitful and destructive marriage relationship. In the former case, the person's life is oriented toward God and the lie was not a good choice. In the latter case, the person's life is based on a lie and so is his or her relationship to the other person. While both missed the mark with their words, the second person is missing the mark with his or her life's fundamental orientation.

Thus, to avoid an individual act and not the life orientation is to treat the symptom and not the disease. Unfortunately some people concentrate only on avoiding sinful acts and forget the fundamental life choices from which the acts flow. Conversely, other people live in great faith in God and yet regard individual acts as making them lost sinners. In the latter case, individual acts become so exaggerated that fundamental life choices for good, honesty, forgiveness and integrity are obscured. Sin is not limited to seven acts of lying but the trajectory of life which shows the patterns in an individual's habitual acts. The axe needs finally to strike the trunk of the tree, not the individual branches. Otherwise the branches will continue to grow.

A better understanding of sin might be given by comparing a person's life to the travel of a moon rocket. The rocket lifts off with enough fuel for propulsion to the moon, (its target), and mid-course corrections. As the rocket moves off target, thrusters compensate for the deviations and bring the rocket back on course. But if the rocket makes a small deviation without a correction, it can go hundreds to thousands of miles off course. If the trajectory changes radically without correction, the rocket becomes lost in space forever with no hope of recovery. So too will be the human person. Little mistakes need to be corrected or they will soon throw the rocket off, possibly by a great margin.

Little sins are never inconsequential. In the history of theology, some called these deviations "venial sins" because, although they dehumanize our relationship with God and others, the trip can still be accomplished. "Mortal sins" were misdirected trajectories whereby people were lost entirely, going somewhere else than they intended, lost in space. Venial sins never added up in a spiritual arithmetic to even one mortal sin. However, one mortal or deadly sin was enough to kill a relationship with God. While mortal and venial were helpful terms to some generations, theology is not bound by these distinctions and now seems to be searching for a clearer relationship between life choices and individual acts. As we will see throughout this book, theology continually renews itself and seeks to understand our faith according to freshly developing insights.

While theology seeks to understand the concept of sin, theologians recognize that this is only half the work. The implications that sin holds for us today need to be addressed. Hence our second concern is the question: what difference does this concept of sin make in our lives? People experience evil all too often. When love breaks down, suspicion rules, hatred and violence become solutions, people use others, despair is encouraged and goodness ridiculed. In short, we experience sin. Deep within everyone is the experience of evil. Of all the theological concepts, it is the least difficult to acknowledge. Yet to completely understand it extends beyond our mind's ability.

For the Christian, Jesus has overcome sin. It has no final victory over us, not even evil's cruelest blow of death. Jesus' death and resurrection have broken its back. The final verdict has been determined. St. Paul exults, "O Death, where is your victory? O death, where is your sting?" (I Cor 15:55) Nevertheless, sin and its effects of evil remain unintelligible, a surd, an enigma. Why do babies die? Why do the innocent suffer? We have no definitive theological answer nor do we run after easy secular answers. The final solution for theology comes from the heart's knowledge that life belongs to God and all have a resting place in God.

Our major task is to avoid being crushed by the evil of sin. The world contains too much suffering. As sinners we contribute to the problem; our challenge is to do good. As we can bring about evil, so can we bring about good, which at times implies the eradication of evil. Individual sin has been the clearest form of sin. Perhaps it stems from the obvious physical responsibility we take for our own bodies' actions in the world. Responsibility for our actions when they are not clearly ours is more ambiguous. Today we are seeking to examine the obscured, physically removed, and less observed effects of our choices.

Two such considerations are: first, sins of omission—we choose to remain "neutral" and avoid the good we are capable of doing; second, structural sins—we participate in structures that harm people or perpetuate such structures. These are sins precisely because we can change the evil that we do, i.e. we know that we support and control these structures by our actions. We can change them. Twentieth century people possess more control over their institutions than before. We know how they work, and we have the power to direct them. Social analysis, modern technology and science have put more power at our disposal, and also more responsibility. Refusing to take the responsibility to change evil situations is sin. As noted before, theology is responding to the insights of the modern world, especially, in this case, the social sciences. This is why sins of omission and structural sin have received more examination in recent decades.

Theology also is stressing an important point: because sin

exists in history, so too will salvation have to come in history. Salvation does not begin in heaven where people are saved but on earth where sin is found. Only when justice flows like water, poverty is resisted, and oppression is removed, will the peace of salvation reign.

As described in this section, this fundamental concept of sin pervades the Christian experience. Sin is less the focus, however, than salvation. We are all called to salvation and the overcoming of sin. Although sin brings the problem, salvation addresses the true goal of humanity.

B. SALVATION

The theological anthropology of the Genesis account begins with the ideal state of humanity symbolized in intimacy with God. Adam and Eve walk and talk with God in an easy personal relationship. From this relationship with God results an easy harmony with all creation, and especially with one another. An idyllic world of peace and love exists. Once the falls occurs and sin enters the world, life consists of a struggle to return to this perfect state. Hence the goal of humanity is the one destined for us from the beginning. In other words, our beginning represents our final destiny. This pursuit of the goal of human life in God is called salvation.

In Genesis, salvation does not refer to life after death or eternal life. To the Old Testament mentality, whether an afterlife existed was a matter of conjecture which one could not solve in this life. That God could continue the life of a person was easily accepted; for, if God could create the world, God could sustain life even after death. Thus salvation was understood to be the pursuit of human goodness in relation to God in the present life. Just as sin entered this world, so did salvation seek to overcome sin *in this world.*

In time, the Jewish faith accepted the possibility of an afterlife, but it was not a teaching that people had to embrace. As we see in the gospel accounts, the Pharisees accepted a resurrection from the dead whereas the Sadducees did not. In Mark's gospel, for instance, Jesus is seemingly trapped by the Sadducees who ask him about the woman whose husband dies and who then marries six more times. Whose wife is she in heaven? The question was directed against the illogical belief in an afterlife. Because Jesus accepted a belief in the afterlife, he resembled the Pharisees. No doubt this argument was a common one used against the Pharisees and shows the strong differences in belief which existed at the time of Jesus.

Rather than speak about an afterlife, Jesus preferred to speak of salvation. He did so in terms of the Kingdom of God. At the beginning of his preaching, Jesus says, "This is the time of fulfillment. The reign of God is at hand. Reform your lives and believe in the gospel." (Mk 1:15) The theme of Jesus' preaching was the Kingdom of God. Salvation was the coming of this Kingdom. It is interesting that Jesus never preached about himself and never demanded people proclaim him as divine. He invited people to see God through his words (e.g. parables) and deeds (e.g. miracles), he taught with God's authority, and he remained obedient to God's will even to death on the cross. This is what the gospels proclaim.

The word "Kingdom" is not one that Americans or many others like to even experience. Kings and kingdoms have negative connotations. But "kingdom" means "rule" or "reign" or "power" of God. Thus we can say that Jesus preached the power of God breaking into the world; or the rule of God taking place; or the reign of God being established in the world. This reign of God was established against the backdrop of sin, evil, and the powers of darkness. "Salvation," which means "safe" or "well being," implies the power of good overcoming the power of evil. Hence the Kingdom of God rescues, redeems, saves, and overcomes. While many words are used to explain salvation as it comes in the Kingdom, they all express the total health, harmony, and peace of the correct relationship with God and creation.

When Jesus healed people, this was a sign of the inbreaking of the Kingdom. In his person Jesus brought the Kingdom; he brought God. With God comes salvation. The name "Jesus" means "God is salvation." Luke uses the title of "savior" for Jesus, Matthew "Emmanuel" (i.e. God-with-us), Mark "Son of God," and John the "Word" made flesh. The richness of these descriptions indicates attempts to understand that the Kingdom was already present in Jesus. The Kingdom is not a thing but a person. Just as we understand God through the richest expression that we know—the human person, so too does God know us and speaks to us through the richest expression that we know—the human person. In Jesus, God and humanity unite in the revelation of who God is for us and who we are for God.

When we believe the good news (gospel), we enter into the Kingdom of God. What is the content of the Kingdom of God? Jesus tells us quite directly: To love God above all things and your neighbor as yourself. This is our one command. Love of God restores the vertical relationship to God that Adam and Eve broke by disobedience. The act of obedience which is faith restores us to the correct relationship with God. Consequent upon the primacy of the relationship with God comes the correct horizontal relationship with one another. According to the Genesis account, belief in God is the key to love of neighbor. In practice, the love of neighbor can lead us to a love of God. The Genesis account only deals with the priorities, and says that no amount of good deeds necessarily restores our relationship with God. This seems to be what Jesus says also. Therefore, one must accept God's Kingdom.

When one accepts God, in faith and obedience, and thereby lives in the Kingdom, what does it imply? Or, in biblical terms, what is God's will for us? The answer is staggering: God has chosen us to be at the center of the Kingdom! Of all the possible plans God could freely devise, God has chosen us to be the center of this deepest love. Who could fathom that when we commit ourselves to God, God turns right around and tells us that what is closest to his heart is that we love one another? The biblical imagery dares to proclaim this deepest truth by proclaiming that we become sisters and brothers related to the same father. Individually and communally, without exception, not even to the exclusion of enemies, we are all at the center of this love. To love God above all requires us to love what God loves which now necessarily implies one another. In theological anthropology's terms, our fullest humanization is in God.

Putting us at the center of his heart is God's free choice. Jesus tells us that it is so. Hence, the Kingdom of God is a love story. God has fallen in love with humanity and will not stay away from us. This love is both that of a parent and a lover. It encompasses every kind of love that humans can experience. It is the greatest story ever told. It seems too good to be true—

unheard of and unexpected. This is good news indeed.

Although the Kingdom of God has come in the person of Jesus, its completion will not arrive until the end of the world. Sin continues to work against salvation. But the victory has already been won. It is like knowing the end of a novel but not knowing the chapters in between. We write these chapters in between. God asks for our participation in the building of that Kingdom. We live it and tell about it to others. Very simply said, this is the role of the church: we are disciples living in God's Spirit and giving witness to others of God's salvation in our lives. We follow the Lord Jesus and await the day of his return. Until then, we live in this "already come but not yet completed" salvation.

The Kingdom of God is not to be understood as a two-layered cake: one layer a natural world down here on earth, and the other layer a supernatural world above. Such duality has no place in Christian thought. Nevertheless, to announce a relationship with God we have often borrowed the image of another world, specifically of heaven, where justice and rewards would abound. By the ambiguity of human language, what began as a spacial image sometimes became spacial reality. Christians were accused of being those focused on a world to come (thus not yet here). Karl Marx described it most poignantly when he called the Christianity of his day an "opiate of the people." He meant that Christianity so pointed to an afterlife where evil would be redressed that it failed to take action in the world and redress the wrongs immediately. Christianity functioned as a narcotic which drugged people to the painful reality oppressing them, offering instead an escape to another world. If Marx were alive today, he might point to Latin American mothers who are told that their babies died because God needed more angels in heaven. The need for additional food and medicine might be a better answer.

At the same time, Marx would be shocked today to see Christianity in places like Latin America, Africa and Southeast Asia calling people to redress evils in this world. Far from being a drug, Christianity has been leading the way in uncovering injustices, oppression, and victimization. Perhaps Marx's stinging criticism has, in the long run, helped us understand the Lord's message. In addition, the reality factor of the Christian message presents a more comprehensive critique of the world than

Marxism. In the end, Marxism may have more reason than Christianity to fear being an opiate.

In the world today, Christianity and Marxism are two of the most powerful voices suggesting the direction that the global nations should go. The vision of the world to come is called a utopia. A utopia is not some ideal vision of the future, like a daydream. Far from it. A utopia speaks about the present and the direction that we should choose in order to be all that we can be. Without a goal, the steps to take in between are unknown. For Christians the Kingdom of God is this utopia, where love, compassion, justice, mercy and peace flourish, and we are brothers and sisters to each other as God made us to be. Unlike Marxism, Christianity does not argue for any particular form of government. Christianity calls for the signs that every government must present, such as justice, compassion, and human dignity, because governments serve humanity. Christianity remains trans-cultural and trans-political.

Unlike Christianity, Marxism has no final solution, only a final state of classless society where all share in the fruits of their labor. Whereas the Marxist utopia is based on a political solution, Christianity is based on human dignity which comes from God and is thereby sacred. Whereas Marxism knows of nothing but the history we make, Christianity understands our history as related to God's Kingdom, which is built upon love. Both understand the arena of the world as the most important place of action. The Christian is no less committed than anyone else, and arguably more committed—because God tells us to love our neighbors and our enemies—to the activities of this world.

The Kingdom of God is a general concept whose particulars are not specified. Like a mansion with many rooms, Christianity offers places for a variety of responses. The fruits of our relating will be the only ways we have to know whether God's reign is in effect. When justice flows like water, when love is the heart of human living and decision making, when compassion extends to everyone, when the poor, the hungry, and the naked are cared for, then we will know the Kingdom has come. From the beatitudes, (straightforward statements of the Kingdom) to the Our Father (where we pray for the coming of the Kingdom), the Kingdom is the center of salvation and the controlling metaphor in Christianity. What it all comes down to is that a hallowed gospel of love that does not bring a removal of oppression and unjust structures is a hollow one. Perhaps this is obvious and need not be explained in detail until our section on church; nevertheless it should be clearly stated: the Kingdom of God is not synonymous with the church. God's rule extends over all creation. The church lives and serves God and his Kingdom, hopefully expressing it in sign, symbol, and sacrament, but the church cannot be identified with the Kingdom. Nor does the church set the Kingdom's limits. Misunderstood or misappropriated sayings such as "outside the church there is no salvation" have no place in God's gift. Salvation certainly exists outside the church for the simple reason that the Kingdom is where God is received. The church struggles to be a living embodiment of this relation with God, holding to the promise of God's Spirit, and inviting others to find the God who loves them.

Throughout the Scriptures, the Kingdom of God is pitted against the kingdom of Satan. Evil reigns in Satan's kingdom. Because God's Kingdom has not yet been completed in history, this world becomes a battle field where both kingdoms vie for humanity in a cosmic clash. However, the victory is assured, the verdict pronounced once and for all: the kingdom of Satan will not prevail, nor shall the gates of hell be open for business as usual. Nevertheless, the fighting continues until the final consummation. In theology, that final consummation is referred to as eschatology ("final age"). Jesus told us that both the present and the future are encompassed in God. Jesus functions as the eschatological prophet who reveals to us both the goal of humanity and, what is extremely important, our eternal identity as loved by God.

What difference does the Kingdom of God make in our lives? The Kingdom of God is not an excuse for people living in this world to ignore one another. Nor is it like a game show where people answer questions to vie for bigger and more expensive prizes. Nor is it a big book with a tally sheet of positive and negative marks. It is empowerment to become more a part of the human condition, and find God there. Salvation empowers us in signs that we recognize. The empowerment is nothing less wonderous than God's very spirit which dwells with us. It is God's freely committed act of graciousness relating us to himself.

For Jesus, the entire act of salvation was so simple: to love God above all and one's neighbor as oneself. This fulfilled the law. This was God's eternal covenant. Instead of being a flight to the supernatural, salvation is a clarion call to become immersed in our total humanity—spiritual, physical, social, political, economic, and cultural.

Some fear that Christianity is becoming too secularized—that is, too worldly. But the word secular means to take what is holy and place it back in the world. From our point of view, that is exactly where God has been calling the church. The holiness of the church is never independent from its universal (catholic) call to evangelization and its brotherhood and sisterhood with all people. The "world" is not an unholy place but the place of salvation. Christianity's greatest challenge is still ahead: will Christians preach and proclaim in word and deed the Kingdom of God's love breaking into people's lives? This relating to God is done through love of God and neighbor. Like God who became flesh and did not stay away from us, we too become enfleshed in this world as Jesus' disciples by the power of God's spirit.

C. FAITH

The third and final building block of theological anthropology is the pursuit of good. In gospel terms, this is called "faith." It relates the human person to the goal of life by overcoming sin. If we think of sin as a downward pull (hell), salvation as an upward pull (heaven), then faith is a forward movement toward salvation (this world and its history). While the concept of faith is simple to understand, the way it functions becomes more complicated and nuanced throughout the history of Judaism and Christianity. Let us begin with the basic concept as it comes from experience and then examine its implications for theology.

The word faith comes from the Hebrew word "emet" which means "to lean on something with all one's weight." The word was used to describe the solid support which held something up. For example, when people of the sandy desert built a house, unless it was built upon something solid like rock, the shifting sand would destroy the house. Faith implied the building of anything upon a solid foundation. In the scriptures, God was often called a rock: "my rock, my salvation"; "my fortress, my rock"; "rock of ages." Jesus finished his sermon on the mountain with a parable of the wise person, in this case the disciple, who built his house upon the firm foundation of rock. To have faith meant that one leaned with all one's weight upon the rock of God who was solid and would not allow one to fall.

People also used the experience of human relationships to explain faith. For example, faith described the experience of a mother holding her baby in her arms. The baby is secure, where she wants to be, comforted, solid. If the baby is taken away from the mother, the baby cries. What is more, Mom won't drop the baby. So too is it with God. Faith means that we rest in the loving embrace of God our parent without fear of being taken, falling, or feeling insecure. God holds each of us solidly. This meaning extends outward to others, e.g. in times of trouble one leans upon a true friend knowing one will not be let down. Faith describes what is solid; the foundation of human life is God and we lean upon him with all our weight.

This same word "emet" has another important derivation. It is the same stem that forms the word "truth." That God is our rock, our solidity and that of the world, is the most basic truth of all creation. To place oneself in God's arms by faith is to make the correct decision, the most truthful act imaginable. Just as a true friend won't let us down, so with God. Our faith is correctly placed in the solid bedrock of truth. Such solidity brings with it the harmony and peace that creation intended. Thus faith describes the basic relation of humanity to God and functions as an important building block for other theological concepts.

If we return to the story of Adam and Eve, humanity broke the correct relationship with God. And with the break, we no longer saw God face to face in intimate friendship. Interestingly, God does not leave the garden and depart for heaven, thereby removing himself from the world. God remains in the garden. It is Adam and Eve who leave, thereby removing themselves from intimacy with God. From this day on, humans will not see God directly. God is hidden from our sight and we are removed from his presence. However, God may elect to be with us outside the garden. Notice that in either case, God remains in this world. Genesis leaves us with a truth that humanity will subsequently live with: we must relate to God as a hidden God. Faith, then refers to what we cannot see but must trust anyway. In sum, life is an act of faith, which is trust. Problems are encountered because, when we cannot see God, we do not know exactly how to relate with him, what to say or do, what he wants for us, whether he is watching us, whether he cares for us. While Genesis describes only Judeo-Christian anthropology, these concerns pervade all religious beliefs.

The re-establishment of the relation with God, then, comes only from God, as a gratuitous gift. God draws near to us. From start to finish, faith remains a free and unmerited gift. But once God offers it, our response creates a relationship in which we lean on God with all our weight, that is totally, without holding back anything. Love calls forth love. This is the truth of human life. To center our lives in anything else is untruth. Genesis has described our life in the twentieth century very accurately and profoundly. Modern experience confirms the truth of the original myth.

The way one leans with all one's weight is less easy to determine. In Judeo-Christian history, one way this kind of relationship was created was through the experience of covenant. In fact, God could be described as a covenant maker. A covenant is a pact, a contract initiated by God, binding himself to us in a certain way, and us to him. In brief, God commits himself to us in a relationship of fidelity. Visible signs accompany the ratification or acceptance of these covenants and seal them as mutual commitments. In time the Old Testament experience revealed that, because God binds himself to the covenant, even if humans break it, God still remains faithful to his side and upholds his covenant forever. God was not toying with humanity. He is so serious about love that he has offered us a second chance for reconciliation. God's fidelity is a solid rock to lean upon forever. His love is everlasting; it never fades or dies.

If we return to the major covenants, God's initiation and fidelity might be more clearly exemplified. After Adam and Eve, God offers a covenant to all humanity in Noah. In the book of Genesis, when God sees that the human race has become so corrupt that nothing can straighten it out, he decides to send a flood and destroy humanity. However, one good man can still be found, so God remains faithful to his creation and offers

Noah a chance to live. Noah builds the ark in obedience to God. Noah leans on God with all his weight and is saved. God sees that the possibility of good still resides in humanity and so he makes a covenant with humanity that he will not destroy them. (This does not imply, however, that we cannot destroy ourselves in a nuclear holocaust!) A rainbow in the sky becomes the sign of that covenant. Every child knows the meaning of the rainbow: when it comes out the rain is over. The point is clear: God has committed himself to the human race and will not forsake us.

This story of Noah is a powerful statement about God's abiding love for us even in the midst of our sin. As the Noah story demonstrates, if love cannot be at the center of our lives, at least obedience can be. Obedience exists simultaneously with the theme of faith and shows what faith is in action. As the Genesis account explains, disobedience on the part of Adam and Eve (sinful action) lead to the introduction of sin. Only through obedience (correct action), done in faith, will the correct relationship with God be restored.

The second covenant is with Abraham, who is the example of the father of faith in three religions: Judaism, Islam, and Christianity. When others hear nothing but silence, Abraham hears a voice. God calls him to leave his possessions in the city of Ur and follow God into the desert, becoming a wandering nomad. Again, an act of faith. This faith leads to further tests of obedience: his wife Sarah who is barren and in old age shall conceive a son whose descendants shall be like the grains of sand on the seashore. Even though Sarah laughs in the tent when she overhears this promise of the three men, no doubt thinking they needed a biology lesson, Abraham believes the impossible. What joy and delight he takes in his son Isaac, born within the year! Then comes the apex of the obedience and act of faith: Abraham is told to take Isaac and sacrifice his life giving it back to God. We can only hear such a command as unthinkable, beyond believability. We ask what kind of God would demand this? Yes, the stakes are the highest, but we have not grasped the seriousness of belief in God, even to the point of the irrational. Abraham has: he believes and obeys. And, as we hoped but could not foresee, at the last moment God sends a messenger, an angel to stop Abraham. The point is not lost on anyone familiar with the Old Testament: as obedience becomes more difficult,

Abraham persists in faith. Or, as Adam and Eve failed in a simple command, Abraham did not fail in a more difficult one. Salvation is beginning anew. A new covenant is established, one of faith wherein God becomes related to Abraham and his descendents in a special way. Its outward sign is the symbolic act of circumcision.

God's covenant with Moses brings the first two covenants together. After the exodus, Moses goes up to the mountain where God offers a new covenant, a new relationship in which he will be their God and they his people. Obedience to the law is the outward sign. In this covenant, we see that God loves people so much that he asks for the relationships which correctly unite him with humanity. The vertical relationship between God and humanity, broken by Adam and Eve, and the horizontal relationship, broken by Cain and Abel, come together in the law. This is not law as we understand it today. This law is a precious gift whereby God reveals the secrets of the correct relationships of the world that were lost with the fall of Adam and Eve. It is a kind of return to their relationship with God in the garden. Like Adam and Eve, Moses even sees God intimately—as intimately as is then possible. Hence the reign of sin is being overcome through the law. This new covenant established the "people of Israel" and binds them to God as a people of faith. This covenant is the one Jesus is born into, lives, and uses to explain God's further covenant.

Notice that a person—or an entire people—lives within several covenants at once, each one deepening the others. Each one deepening a relationship with God. Whereas the theme of the fall is strong in theology, it is not the only interpretation of the relationship. One could just as easily say that God wants to come closer and closer to the human heart. God so loves the world that, like a passionate lover, he cannot stay away. In each covenant, God offers humanity a closer and fuller relationship to himself. Matthew, in the gospel, goes so far as to call Jesus "Emmanuel"—God with us. The history of the human race is a love story. God pursuing and wooing; ourselves pursued and wooed. It is easy to see God's activity as characteristically masculine in this activity; he is the aggressive suitor.

In the new covenant with Jesus, God further commits himself to us. Not in the law but in his spirit that dwells within us. God has now chosen to deal with us directly through the Spirit. The barrier between ourselves and God is gone forever. The law of obedience becomes the law of love, with God's spirit as the dynamic source. The Kingdom comes.

In the gospels, the obedience of Jesus as the one who both knows and does the will of the Father is the perfect attunement to God that Adam and Eve sought. The faith of Jesus is a perfect and total leaning upon God; the Son knows the heart of his Father and obeys it. Divinity and humanity unite in this love affair, and become the model of our discipleship. God promises his enduring love with Jesus' life and death, and sends his spirit who continues to dwell within us through our faith and obedience.

Hope

Because God is the faithful rock, our truth and our support, we can be sure of his constancy. This certainty of faith is the basis of Christian hope. Hope does not see what is hoped for, nor does it completely possess the object of its desire; but it does possess part of it and knows that the rest will arrive. Hope is a purchase on the future that calls for a transformation of the present. We know in faith that God will not be denied his victory.

From what we desire now because of faith—a small taste of how good these relations are now—we hope for their final completion and consummation. The theology of hope, and liberation theology as well, have emphasized the God of hope who can enter sinful situations, empower us to liberation, and bring about the Kingdom. This rediscovery of the power of hope has been an important theological contribution in recent decades. Without hope, humanity shrivels up and dies. Sin cannot be overcome. Evil wins. A God who gives us hope is a God who calls for change and transformation that we can participate in. Marx would be stunned to learn that in many places in the world a God of hope galvanizes people's involvement in society and leads the call to human dignity.

Love

Faith and hope give way to love. A God who calls us to himself, who becomes more and more involved with us, who will be faithful to us, forgives us, reconciles us, is a God who loves. A. N. Whitehead called him a "fellow sufferer who cares." While it is difficult to imagine a God with a human heart who loves as we do, it is more than true. Whatever human love is, it is "seen in a glass darkly" what God's even more immense love is for us. Human love, in other words, is an imperfect, scaled-down version of God's love. If we think we know love, we know something of God who is love. We will be even more overwhelmed by the fullness of this love when we are born again at our deaths.

This love of God is gratuitous. God did not have to love us at all, and certainly not with such passion. We can speak of a passionate God even though we know God does not have passions like we do (e.g., anger). Nevertheless, the history of salvation reveals a God who comes to us, relentlessly, without condition or warning. We can only describe such a strong love, a love that overcomes rationality and will not take "no" for an answer, as passion. The Song of Songs in the Old Testament captures the truth of God's passionate love affair with humanity. I would also like to say that there are no strings attached, that the passion is God's problem but that would be incorrect. While God does not force us, he does continue to give us the freedom to love him or not, just as he did with Adam and Eve. Hence God's passion is our problem. God wants us to accept his love and love him in return because it is best and truest for us. In brief, love is the center of human life. It is because of this truth that Jesus told us so straightforwardly what God's heart is all about: God loves us and, to paraphrase the great theologian Augustine, our hearts will be restless until they rest in loving him.

At the heart of life is not just any kind of love, but an involving love relationship with both God and neighbor. The relationship is what matters. For example, one can love without return, as a mother loves her child. The love comes first from the mother, before the child can respond. But when the child becomes an adult and loves mom back, then love becomes a reciprocal relationship. The relationship where the child is loved and loves, where mom is loved and loves, becomes the ideal. A give-and-take situation is not love. One gives and takes for the sake of the love relationship: one initiates and receives love for the sake of both people. Because we are committed to a loving relationship, each of us grows in mutual relationship with the other, both giving and receiving. One does what is best for the mutual love relationship, not for my loving or your loving. Both persons grow in the total relationship of love. One speaks, or listens, gives or takes, according to what will enhance the relationship. Not my love or your love but *our* love relationship becomes the issue. I-thou becomes we.

Faith, hope, and love are the three great theological virtues that express the one relationship with God and the forward movement of this ongoing relationship. From these, all others flow, adding dimensions of understanding to our relationship with God. For example, the virtue of justice flows from these three. Justice is not our justice but God's. Judgment about the worth of others does not come from their financial worth, status, power, or attractiveness. Justice extends to every person, even when they do not "deserve" it. The dignity of human persons is not self-evident or we would not treat people the way we do. Racism, sexism, and cultural imperialism are three cases in point: they exist, and they must be resisted. Human dignity is something that we must fight for, even when dehumanizing injustices seem more like normal fare. God calls forth a justice forged with love and not duty, right or might. The extra mile is walked, the extra tunic given, the offense pardoned even seventy times seven. One gives from one's want and not solely from one's abundance. The neighbor is loved even if he is the enemy. In other words, no border line or limiting case can be an endpoint for our loving. Justice then abounds because love abounds. The Law of an eye for an eye cannot continue; someone must blink. Right must not claim its pound of flesh. These are hard words but they are salvific words, with real power behind them. God's justice is founded upon love, and we can participate in that just love with every action.

D. INVITATION AND CONVERSION

The basic concepts of sin, salvation, and faith do not drop down like rain from above. They have emerged from the most profound and deeply human experiences in contact with God, others, and self. They can never be the exclusive property of one person, group, or religion; they belong to everyone. The missioning statement of Jesus to go forth to the entire world and preach this good news simply reflects the truth that the Christian experience holds for everyone. Hence, missioning is at the heart of the believer. Yet theologians recognize that the Christian believer's connectedness with God precedes the missioning. Nevertheless, not all are believers nor do they share this same faith. The question arises then as to how God speaks to us. For the Christian, we have a history, a tradition, a story that expresses how God has dealt with us. Taken in a wider sense of every human person, the manner of speaking to us is not exclusively Christian but belongs to every human person. It is, therefore, normative rather than exclusivist. It expresses one

Invitation

As the covenants reveal, God loves human persons both as individuals and as part of humanity in general. From Adam and Eve in the garden to Abraham in front of his tent, Moses at the burning bush, David tending his flock, Amos pruning his sycamores, Isaiah in a vision, the virgin Mary going about her chores, and even Jesus at his baptism, God calls out to us. The image of call is a strong one in Christianity and is rendered in Latin as vocation ("vocare" to call). Vocation has two meanings in theology, the initial call of the Christian to belief and, secondly, the ongoing call to serve the Lord by following some occupation. Both indicate God's luring of the individual to discipleship.The great modern theologian Karl Rahner seized upon this openness to God's call and spoke of human beings as "hearers of the word." Of couse, "word" has two meanings: the word spoken by God and then the WORD, or logos, Jesus himself. Humans are open to God's word which, when spoken most intimately and in the flesh, is Jesus.

God acts, communicates, involves himself in our lives and

then intertwines us with one another. When we hear the voice that overtakes us, we possess the freedom to respond with a yes or no—whether hearty or half-hearted. Unlike any other word, God's call cuts deeply, like a two-edged sword, to the heart of who we are. It demands nothing less than a total yes, an involving and intertwining yes. We know that we are not alone, that God invites us to a fuller life, and that we must trust this relationship. Empowerment, called grace, ensues from this relationship—Rahner called grace "God's self-communication." We do not receive a thing but a person. Grace is not a package of white holy dust, it is entering into a relationship with God himself.

The call-response analogy speaks about the manner of this relating. It is active and dynamic, awesome and fascinating, engaging and indissoluably mysterious. As all good human relationships testify, the head will never finally figure out the reasoning of the heart. One does not reason to love, one falls in love with another. The call of God is most basically an invitation to fall in love. The continued calls beckon us to cooperate even more fully with love, falling deeper in love. The theologian Bernard Lonergan described this discipleship as "Being-in-love," a play on the word "being" as philosophically implying that all exists in God, and disciple as the concrete, historical expression of that interacting love. He refers to the developing relationship as a call to ongoing conversion, a concept we will examine later in this chapter.

The call-response metaphor is not a one-directional act in which one speaks and the other listens. It is a conversation in which the mutual good of both becomes the most important consideration for both parties. One speaks and listens, initiates and receives, according to the development of the love relationship. It is not a question of doing everything for the other person at my expense. That is one-directional. Rather it is a two-way street of mutual love, respect, concern, care, and hopes, where both grow in who they are. As great as God is, he respects, frees, and loves us more than we do ourselves. The call-response metaphor requires mutual loving because God desires it that way. Happily but surprisingly, it is God's way that most enhances our own humanity.

Although it might seem so, the call-response metaphor is not a two-step process of God calling and us responding. Instead, because of its mutuality, it is a three-step process: (1) informing (2) conforming (3) transforming. The evangelists Luke and John found the unparalleled call-response metaphor in Mary the mother of Jesus. For Christians today, she represents the first disciple. Mary's call and response exhibits the three-step process of all discipleship. Let us examine this calling in detail from Luke's gospel.

(1) The word of God addressed Mary by name, i.e., personally. The angel Gabriel, God's messenger, tells Mary she is to be the mother of a son, Jesus. God's plan is put before her in the initial invitation. Mary is respected, invited, freed, and loved. Once having heard God's invitation, she is free to either accept or reject the motherhood offered. She does not understand how this could be and so questions Gabriel. A conversation takes place. Gabriel reveals more and more of God's plan to Mary. God both speaks and listens through Gabriel in the mutuality of the newly forming relationship. Having heard the information, Mary is ready to respond.

(2) Mary conforms to the word spoken. She asks that it be done to her as Gabriel says. Her yes, or fiat, changes the relationship. She now becomes a partner in God's desire which means becoming the mother of Jesus. God asks her to conform to his call. It implies a commitment to the relationship and sacrifices. Specifically for Mary it means motherhood. Her life changes to conform to the decision she has made. Mary becomes pregnant, and her life is never the same once Jesus enters. No matter what our call is, we will be asked to incarnate God in our lives as Mary did. As the prototype of every disciple, she represents both literally for herself and figuratively for us the one who hears the word of God and conforms to it. The living out of her conformation remains to be done.

(3) Mary's life changes because of God's invitation. She has heard the word, has conformed her life to it, and now becomes transformed by it. A new set of relationships develops which she will live for the rest of her life. Most specifically, Jesus is her son and Joseph her husband. Mary is still Mary but she has "crossed over" (trans) into a new way of living (formed). She lives from and in this new relation with God which involves her in God's love and intertwines her in the lives of others. Without knowl-

edge of the future and without imposing conditions, she transforms these relationships into the loving expression of her one-
time yes. Her call and response is both ongoing and complete: it
transforms every person and event she experiences. Her conformation is tested in the crucible of living out the relationship
formed. If she had not accepted the call (she was, after all, free
to choose) or if she had decided that motherhood was too
demanding, then the three-stage process would have fallen apart.
But so too would it have fallen apart if she had refused to
continue the call in the transformative stage. Thus it is not
enough to say yes; one must conform one's life to that yes, and
then live this transformed life in and from a mutual relationship
with God.

The reason for explicating the three-step process is to emphasize that the call of God entails ongoing conversion from the
start. Faith is not static but processive, moving, changing, developing, restructuring. The God of mystery and surprise re-
makes and refashions the involvement of the relationship. This
God both involves us with himself and intertwines us with one
another in greater ways. Once part of this passionate love affair,
our lives call forth greater faith (leaning on God) and greater
obedience (acts of love).

Conversion

The informing-conforming-transforming stages of God's invitation to us emphasize the need for ongoing conversion, one of
the most discussed topics in theology today. It involves both the
missionary efforts into other cultures and the ongoing conversion
of every Christian. The presupposition at work is that faith is
dynamic, not static, and calls forth further conforming to the
word of God which results in further transformation. Let us
begin with why people become Christian and then continue with
models of conversion, both personal and social. We will begin in
human experience and then move to interpretive models of
personal and social conversion.

Many different starting points exist for conversion. We can
use the image of a pilgrimage by the human race to a mountain
top. Everyone begins from a different departure point, and
everyone faces a different journey depending upon the terrain to

be covered, and thereby makes provisions depending upon whether hills or desert lie ahead. For example, desert people do not need heavy furs. They also will not envision a God of colder regions, but one who speaks to their desert terrain. Each starting point is the religious sentiment of the human race, some in organized religions, others in revealed religions. The Christian knows that the mountain top is accessible to all and that the Christian already possesses knowledge of the journey. In a word, the Kingdom of God has already broken upon the Christian consciousness, not as a badge of pride but as a responsibility to help everyone on their individual journeys to God.

For the Christian, many different starting points exist for the conversion experience where one "turns with" God and leans upon him with all one's weight. Just a few of these starting points are:

(1) Some people are Christians because of their personal experience of being loved by God. They do not start from scripture, philosophy, or doctrine but from their own histories.

(2) Some start from the experience of forgiveness, prayer, or the acceptance of themselves before God for who they are.

(3) Some begin from the commitment of a family that prays and worships together. They experience church as a wholesome expression of the family's love. As Rahner said, the family really is the most basic building block of the church.

(4) Others believe because of tragedy, whether the loss of a loved one, a divorce, an alcoholic problem, or personal sickness. A change in their life occurs because they are no longer in control.

(5) Others happen into an event by accident, e.g., they make a retreat or go on a Teens Encounter Christ (TEC) weekend, or a cursillo. Sometimes they encounter situations of poverty, oppression, or simply the chance to serve others.

(6) Others are forced to make major decisions, e.g., a career move, a value to be lived, a moral choice. They are forced to make a decision which plummets them back to their most basic reasons for belief.

(7) Others find in Jesus a model, someone to be imitated and followed in moral example. They desire to be good, upright, and

just people who hope for a better world. Christ is their goal in life.

(8) Others are raised Christian and choose to remain so without great upheaval. Their faith seems as natural as the air they breathe and supports them in good and bad times.

For some, belief is easy. For others, it is a struggle. No two people are the same. William James provided an interesting insight when he spoke about conversions from a psychological point of view. He determined that some were "once born" and found life easy; others were "twice-born" and found life exacted decision after decision from them. James found the twice-born the healthiest because they knew both sides and therefore made better informed choices at greater expense.

Alcoholics Anonymous, though not Christian per se, has served many in their Christian conversion experiences. The insight provided is that one must rely upon a greater, higher power. One cannot pull oneself up by one's own bootstraps. Only with the help of one greater than us can we draw the strength to live one day at a time. Many find a parallel here to the Christian God who is greater than us, who sustains us, and who cares for our well-being (salvation).

From various personal experiences of conversion, let us move to elaborated and organized models of conversion operative in theology.

The dominant model of personal conversion belongs to Bernard Lonergan. Beginning from the act of understanding which he finds common in all human experience, he sketches a four-fold conversion. There are intellectual, moral, affective, and religious conversions. The first three correspond to our abilities to know, will, and feel. Turning these to a power beyond ourselves is a religious conversion. The four levels are integrated. If a conversion occurs on the intellectual level, for example, it will influence the others to become integrated. Likewise, a moral conversion will require the others to become integrated. The process is total, ongoing, authentic, and integrative. Lonergan's insight is the deciphering of the four dimensions of personal conversion. He maintains that if the act of understanding proceeds with its integrity, these four conversions join together, reaching for a totality.

Lonergan has established a model for interpreting conversion.

Whether or not his act of understanding can truly undergird the conversion process is still being debated. Whether or not it bears this weight logically, I believe that as a genuine insight into the 4-fold conversion process it will stand on its own. Lonergan has related four different dimensions of every conversion and has shown us the process of continual conversion.

For example, to return to Mary as our call-response paradigm, the information, or intellectual level, called Mary to a new affective, moral, and religious conversion. She changed totally in her choices, her emotions, and her relationship with God. We can imagine that, had Mary become pregnant without God's invitation first, she would have undergone an intellectual conversion secondly, after the event.

That some people experience belief as difficult to understand should not trouble us unduly. Nor should we provide answers as if it is a matter of finding the right one. The conversion process is more respectful of the individual's process of conversion. The individual has faith and is struggling to integrate it. The other levels may be fine and strong, with only the intellectual dimension seeking resolution. The same holds for the other dimensions. For example, one who struggles with going to church on Sunday may be struggling to integrate on the moral dimension what he or she knows, feels, and is religiously involved in. Lonergan's model does not allow for easy judgments about others; rather it holds their process in greater respect. It also provides a way of dealing with others by respecting their growth in faith and the unique way the Lord calls them. This model also calls people to a total conversion where head, heart, will, and belief come together. Struggle is acceptable and necessary in the conversion process.

While Lonergan's model deals with personal conversion, it is not enough. The kingdom of God is both within us and outside of us. Lonergan's model needs the completion that a social model of conversion can provide.

A model of social conversion needs to be developed in theology. Of late, theology has become aware of the macro structures that contextualize and determine our human options. A complete liberation of the human person requires social structures that contribute to human dignity. While the following model is not intended as a final solution, it does present the full range of social responsibility of the disciple in the world today. "To pick up one's cross" as a disciple means to embrace these four dimensions of reality: backward, forward, inward, and outward. These comprise the "cross of reality."

1. Backward refers, of course, to the past. It implies two thousand years of Christian tradition inserted into an even longer historical tradition wherein we find ourselves today. We are born into the middle of a story that continually unfolds. Hence the weight of that tradition rests upon us. We are believers within that tradition and we possess a communal identity. The disciple is not free to discard this tradition and the identity which flows from it: whether scriptural, doctrinal, or ecclesial. Because we are constantly being recreated in continuity with our past, we Christians have long memories that speak of God's continued interaction with us. If we are to respond as a disciple today, we cannot betray our past.

2. Forward refers to the future. It implies that Christians do not stand still like settlers but move ever onward like pioneers. We journey through life with feet solidly set upon the earth, seeking the Kingdom of God where love reigns and empowers everything. Hence Christians are people of hope who depend upon the re-creative action of the Holy Spirit to make all things new. The disciple proclaims this forward transformation of life in love as the purpose of all we do.

3. Inward refers to the individual. It implies that God has given us primary responsibility over our own selves. We make the decision either to center everything in our life in God, or not. Our physical body, our psychological and emotional life, and our spirit comprise the inward dimension. These too are influenced by other factors such as family, chemicals, disease, temperament, and love. Hence being a Christian implies being totally in touch with the various dimensions of what constitutes this human being, in order to hand everything of the self over to the Lord. The disciple is a believer who continually works on this inward dimension of handing his or her very self totally over to the Lord.

4. Outward refers to other people and events. It implies all the social relationships which comprise human life. The word "culture" means "to nourish." As a farmer cultivates his field, so do we cultivate our minds, feelings, and interpersonal relations

in the form of institutions. No one is an island and Christian belief never stops with the individual. It is thoroughly corporate, first in the belief community we call church and secondly in the connectedness of the human family as brothers and sisters. The command of Jesus to love God above all else necessarily implies the love of neighbor. Hence being a Christian requires us to share our life and to care for one another. This neighborly care comes in the form of just social institutions and the interpersonal dealings.

Embracing the inward, outward, backward and forward dimensions of life, the disciple picks up this "cross of reality" daily and follows Jesus. Each dimension can only be interpreted through Jesus' cross, through his identity as the son of God and his role in our present situation. The disciple learns from his or her master. The disciple's challenge is to integrate the past, future, individual and social responsibilities into this present moment. While the invitation has been made, the response and then the continual life-long conversion is ours to make. It is the spirituality of every disciple; it is faith in action.

2

The Content of Theology

1. The Basic Relationships: Jesus, God, and Us

In Part I, we discussed the basic building blocks of theology. These included the formative ideas from which subsequent theological discourse continues: for example, faith, salvation, kingdom of God, tradition, conversion, language, culture, and anthropology. No matter if one changes the words, the realities that these convey must be considered by any theology. Not only do they describe the basic relationship between ourselves and God in our tradition, but they also express recurring dimensions of our experience.

In Part II, we wish to enter into the heart of theology: the understanding of Jesus, God, and us. These three realities circumscribe all theological efforts. In fact, theology could be said to be a search for the understanding of these three realities and their relationship to one another. As three interrelated concepts, they each make sense in terms of the others. No two can be separated off by themselves, e.g., just God and Jesus, or Jesus and us, or God and us. Christianity understands each to be distinct but always related to the others. The task of theology is to understand this triad and its relevance to faith.

Throughout this book, our method has been to rediscover theology from the inside out. We have begun with experience—first of the person (theological anthropology) and then extending outward to the basic theological concepts which we referred to as the building blocks upon which other theological concepts depend. We will continue to work from experience, but with a slightly different twist.

Because Jesus, God and human persons form the central relationships of theology, we will take each in turn, present the topic (area it covers, history, importance, and current state of affairs), and then ask what difference it makes to us today. First we ask the nature and content of theology (what is it?), and then we ask its implications and importance to life today (what difference does it make?). In this way, the topics will not float disconnected from life as if in some intellectual outer space—a danger with all abstracted understanding. Instead, we will attempt to indicate the important consequences these ideas have upon human living.

When theological doctrine has been written about in the past, the content has proceeded logically according to importance: first God, then Jesus, then the Church, and then us. But in our experience, we really begin with Jesus, then God, and finally their relation to us as Church. Because Jesus is the key to the interpretation of our experience, we will follow this latter procedure. While this approach is not the ordinary one, it does more clearly indicate the centrality of Jesus as the source for our interpretation of our experience.

A. JESUS

The experience of Christian faith rests upon who Jesus was, what he said and did, and how he was experienced by the early disciples. I will refer to this complex of relationships as "the Jesus event." Our theology is specifically called Christian because of the revelation given by and in Jesus. Although the Judaic tradition also forms part of the Christian tradition of belief, nevertheless the Jesus event interprets both the pre-Christian events and all subsequent Christian tradition. One would not be overstating its importance by saying that Jesus is essential to Christian belief and therefore to theology. Jesus becomes the interpreter of God, and also of us. Thus even our understanding of God is illuminated by the Jesus event and rightly follows after our study of this event. Whether explicitly or implicitly, every question about God or us raises the question of Jesus. But how are we to understand the Jesus event?

In the wide sense of the word, Christology forms the central,

systematized body of knowledge about Jesus. It does not exhaust
the meaning and implication of Jesus, nor the experiences of
people over thousands of years and around the globe.

Where does our knowledge of the Jesus event come from?
Usually it begins in the ordinary experiences of our lives. Some
may find it in a personal experience of love, forgiveness, acceptance, awe, the holy, suffering, or belongingness, to mention
only a few ways. These experiences are the most basic to human
living and remain below the surface of our constant attention.
As unexplicated but no less faith, these experiences undergird
our whole lives. Because they are so much of who we are, to
examine them is to touch the deepest level of our faith. When
theology examines faith, these experiences are the ones addressed
and made explicit. Then the work of theology is truly engaging
our faith. Defined as faith seeking understanding, theology
articulates these faith experiences. Because Christology studies
who Jesus is and what differences he makes in our lives, in its
widest sense, Christology opens the door to religious understanding, confirming our experiences as truly Christian. Thus
Christology is both explanative of who Jesus is and indicative of
the difference he makes in our lives.

Christology gathers up the wisdom of the tradition, all the
sources and resources that one can draw upon, and enters into
conversation with our understanding of the Jesus event. Thus
one measures the authenticity of one's own experience with the
continuous thread of the Christian experience over 2000 years.
There is continuity of religious experience despite the discon-
tinuity of people, ages, circumstances, and stages of spiritual
growth. Each Christian can say, "This is my experience too."
We not only identify an experience as truly Christian, but
continue to shape, mold, and develop that same Christian
experience into the future. No one believes the same way. On
our own, each of us unique, different from all the others yet
emerged from a common tradition, we enter the uncharted
waters of the future. There we will continue to find the Jesus
event alive and nourishing. Still leaning upon God with all our
weight, we follow him into this future.

What is this Jesus event? How does it become a measure of
my own experience of faith?

The Jesus event begins in the experience of the first disciples.

They witnessed Jesus' life and death. They retold the story of God coming to them in the form of Jesus. The New Testament writings, especially the four gospels, form our earliest recorded experiences of faith. Does one say experiences (plural) because so many individual and communal experiences have been intertwined? Or does one say experience (singular) because it was the one same Lord that they experienced? Let us call it experience to emphasize our common participation.

In scholastic theology, the resurrection event was considered the foundation of Christian belief. As Paul said, "If Jesus has not risen from the dead, then our faith is vain." But scholastic theology did not use modern scripture studies with their new historical-critical methods. Today the resurrection is understood in light of Jesus' entire life. We cannot reduce the Jesus event to Jesus resurrected any more than we can limit it to Jesus as a living person. The life, death, and resurrection of Jesus form an unbreakable unit. This is why the term "Jesus event" is preferred to "resurrection event."

In the nineteenth century, attempts were made to find the "historical Jesus," i.e. the true Jesus behind the written texts. This pursuit failed. It was impossible to get behind the texts and, by extension, the tradition of faith. The inability to get behind the text presented difficulties for developing biblical exegesis. Hermeneutics, or the principles of interpretation, sought a solid starting point at least in the text itself, but even this proved incomplete. One must also deal with the reception of the texts as authentic by the Christian community. We might refer to this explosive potential in the text as narrative theology. Therefore, interpretation of texts rests both with the biblical exegete and the theologian. A fuller discussion of this problem is outside the scope of this study; however, we will return to the nature of texts in a later chapter.

If one takes the writing of the gospels as occurring in 65 (Mark), 75 (Luke), 85 (Matthew), and 90 (John), as commonly accepted, then one is dealing with over 35 years of development and fluid tradition by the time of the first gospel, and more than 60 years for the last gospel. Furthermore each gospel differs from the others on many accounts. Thus, to render a historically accurate picture of Jesus in some objective way without presupposing the earliest disciples' belief seems impossible. Of course there does remain the possibility of earlier texts being discovered, but that would present problems with their authenticity since these documents were not preserved by the early church. We can cross that bridge when we come to it.

To summarize a great deal of material, the scriptures provide the earliest witness and explanation of the Christian experience. Christology is irrevocably rooted in this source. If all the bibles in the world were destroyed, as Christians we would go back and record them from memory. We would retell the stories of Jesus because he remains normative for our Christian experience today. But if we could not remember the stories, we would have to write the present experiences that we have and collect them, and by necessity elevate them to the status of a norm so others could come in contact with the Christian experience as authentically lived. Our experiences would become a type of norm because they would be the closest point of contact to the witness of Jesus in our tradition.

The gospels themselves might have been written under such conditions. The original eye-witnesses like Peter and John and the one born out of time, Paul, were dying ("martyr" means "witness" to the faith) or growing old. These may have been concerns that prompted them to record their witness. Note that only two of the gospels have apostles' names connected to them by tradition—Matthew and John. Luke and Mark were other, perhaps later, disciples. Other circumstances surely surrounded the writing of the gospels—perhaps concerns about the authenticity of the tradition, or need to correct misguided interpretations or provide the many new Christian communities with knowledge of the Jesus event. Nevertheless, that the gospels were written at all remains a marvel. That these four works capture the Jesus event, *the* gospel, so authentically remains God's gracious gift to us.

The Jesus event tells us who God is: one who loves us, cares for us, and relates to us in forgiveness and compassion. God is one who desires to draw nearer to us and bring us nearer to him. God is for us.

The Jesus event tells us who we are: ones loved by God, who are to love God and neighbor even to the extent of loving our enemies. We are for God.

The Kingdom of God that Jesus preached puts God at the

center of our faith. We love God above all things, above all creatures, even above ourselves. But what is it that God loves and desires? Here is where God astounds us. God has freely chosen us as the center of his love and desire. To love God means to love our neighbor as ourselves. God's cause is our cause. God and humanity come together in the Kingdom of God. Nothing and no one is excluded. Responding to God's cause drives us deeper into our humanity and into our relation with God. Responding to our neighbor drives us deeper into our humanity and our relation with God. Love says it all. But not just any kind of love. The love that Jesus offered was self-giving, reconciling, serving, and compassionate. Jesus shows us, in word and action, how to love God and neighbor.

The humanity of Jesus was obvious to his disciples. Jesus was like them. The divinity of Jesus was something they eventually came to understand, especially after his death. By the time of John's gospel, the divinity of Jesus is expressed strongly from the beginning in the Word (Logos) of God made flesh. But in all four gospels, divinity remains the harder concept to grasp. Understanding Jesus as both human and divine has long been a problem for theology. In faith it may be easier to accept than to explain. But theology seeks to understand and explain this mystery as best it can. Many controversies and hard feelings have been caused over various interpretations. The disputes have not been inconsequential. Without trying to provide an actual theology, I would like to offer an *interpretive model* for understanding the various theologies, and hence the controversies. Through this pedagogical model, the parameters of the various theologies can be located and the various conclusions made more understandable. Hopefully, this will help us contextualize the various controversies and avoid the same problems in the future.

An interpretive model that serves to explain the divine-human relationship of Jesus is called "high and low" Christology. These are spatial images. High means one begins with the divinity of Jesus and descends from above to the humanity of Jesus. Various other words describe the same reality and are sometimes used interchangeably: descending Christology, or Christology from above. The other category is low Christology where one begins with the humanity of Jesus and ascends to the divinity of

Jesus. Correlative terms for low Christology are: ascending Christology, or Christology from below. The distinctions are starting points, not exclusive references. Even if one begins in a high Christology, one must still explain Jesus' humanity. Even if one begins with low Christology, one must explain Jesus' divinity. Thus, while one enters the lake from only one spot, one can get out on the other side. If one begins in high or low Christology, one must swim to the other side to complete the understanding. The reason is simple: Jesus shows us the Father and shows us who we are. We cannot separate the unique relation of Jesus as the Son of God from his humanity as one like us. Like two sides of the one same coin, high and low Christology are inseparable in the person of Jesus. Theology distinguishes the two for the purpose of understanding the humanity-divinity parameter which shapes Christian theology.

This distinction was most clearly expressed in the great christological councils of the fourth and fifth centuries. The council of Chalcedon (451) finally expressed it as an article of Christian faith that Jesus was truly God and truly man, not 50-50 but 100% God and 100% man. This teaching is remarkably restrained and clear about the Christian experience. The vocabulary of person and nature, and the anthropology that they used, can be improved upon. But the council's expression of the reality of Jesus' relation to the Father and us remains at the center of our belief.

Because Chalcedon used the divine-human categories, the high/low Christology model provides a helpful interpretive understanding of the subsequent controversies and proposed Christologies. A complete history remains the work of another volume but the main parameters of the controversies and solutions (doctrines) are understandable already.

From the time of John's gospel, high Christology has dominated theology. That Jesus was human was apparent; how he revealed God's very self and our relation to God was new. By the twentieth century, Jesus' divinity dominated the equally true statement of his humanity. It was as if the other half of the Chalcedonian doctrine had been forgotten. Only in the last several decades (inspired in part by new theological anthropology) have we begun to recover Jesus' humanity in low Christology, principally through the recent work in scripture studies. The balance has not been achieved: more work on the humanity of Jesus remains to be done. But the prospects are good, because a redressing of both low and high Christology is not being done apart but together simultaneously. The future seems open to many new developments in Christology, including a return to the sources of scripture and tradition to retrieve the richest deposits of our Christian experience.

Further considerations: what difference does Jesus make?

The high/low model for Christology helps us locate the starting point of various theologies. Rooted in conciliar documents and in the earliest Christian experience of our tradition, this model provides a corrective to every theology by pointing out that both realities must be present. While no theology can do everything, every theology must admit its presuppositions and limitations. As said above, the model provides the parameters of theological discussion, not the content. The Chalcedonian doctrine opened the door to further exploration by setting parameters: Jesus is divine and human. This doctrine does not close theological discussion.

Recent theologies have challenged the adequacy of the high/ low model. Derived from contemporary experience, these theologies raise the question of what difference a high or low Christology makes to the believer? The question can be rephrased this way: high/low Christology concerns itself with *who* Jesus is. One might say the nature of Jesus is paramount. But these new theologies, such as liberation theology, ask about the relation of Jesus to us: *what difference* does Jesus make to our world today? Another element is needed to complete traditional Christology. One might call this corrective an *action* Christology, as David Tracy does. For one lives the Christian faith and finds in committed action the disclosive power of the Jesus event.

The image of the disciple represents this model well. In discipleship, the believer follows Jesus on a journey. One leans with all one's weight upon the sustaining power of one's relationship with God. Everything comes from and flows out of this relationship. One seeks understanding, and seeks to translate that understanding into deeper, committed faith. The disciple does not ignore the levels of conversion of the "cross of reality." Life becomes a call to deeper love and to trust in even more love. There cannot be too much. In imitation of Christ, the disciple follows the Lord on a journey through life. This journey is the action of love whereby the Kingdom of God becomes a reality. It is not enough to know love, one must give and experience love. Words and deeds go together. Matthew expresses it well at his scene of the Last Judgment, when one is judged by whether one gave water to the thirsty, food to the hungry, clothes to the naked... Discipleship requires both words and deeds.

Following Jesus as divine is impossible; we are human and can only be human. We must enter into Jesus' life through his humanity. In our age, the agonizing question is not whether God exists. Rather it is whether God cares: does God make a difference in my life? Do I make a difference to God? In Jesus, God's caring is manifested. As one like us, as one who dies on the cross and who lives in close association with the Father, Jesus tells us that God cares and is intimately bound up with us. We are his cause, his concern, his love.

This dimension of Christology has not come forward with enough strength. If theology is going to speak to people today, to their experiences, to their hopes and dreams, to their fears and sufferings, then the relevancy or relationality of God to these experiences needs to be explored. For the future, theology needs to attract theologians who can explore and articulate for others a Christology about the difference God makes in our lives. The pastoral concern of theology today has been a great help in bringing Christology forward to action.

Christology is continuing to return to Scripture for better understanding of Jesus, his work, his mission. Through the new scriptural advancements, the entire history of Christology can be reinterpreted with the high/low/action model. As one might expect, Christology has become a fast-paced discipline in theology because every dimension of theology is related to Jesus. The heart of every theological statement touches upon Jesus in some way. Thus the future will be just as fast-paced, and new understandings of ourselves and God will continue to develop.

B. GOD

Jesus brings us to the Father. The self-communication of God comes through Jesus. The revelation of God in Jesus is not an exclusive entrance to salvation, but it is a privileged one. From the earliest creation to many areas of the globe today, people have never heard of Jesus and yet journey toward salvation. As the genesis mythos indicates, all creation comes from and, even in sin, remains related to God. Vatican II explicated this connectedness to God by saying that people of good will who follow their consciences are saved. Rather than taking away the mission of the church, this statement affirms that we have no need to devise ways of keeping people away from God. Instead, we are missioned to find ways of bringing people more fully to him.

Jesus brings people to God and God to people. Those who follow him in discipleship bring people to Jesus to the Father and the Father to Jesus to us. Rather than imagining ourselves as owners of faith, we might think of ourselves as brokers: we try to help others find God in their lives and let God communicate with them. In this way, disciples serve God in the manner of Jesus.

In the theology practiced until Vatican II, the topic of God began discussion. Theology probed and sought to prove the existence of God. Once that was done, it advanced to the topic of Jesus as the divine one sent by God. Finally theology examined the church, established by Jesus, from which we receive our faith. This sequence of theological topics began in God and ended in our faith, each step building upon the previous one. In fact, the image of a building was used, and the process was referred to as "fundamental theology."

In the Christian life experience, the process is just the opposite. We do not begin with God and work down to faith; we begin in faith and work upward to God. We do not stop at Jesus. Faith becomes the context in which the revelation of Jesus is verified and lived out. In other words, understanding comes from faith, not faith as the result of a series of proofs. (Then one would have a God who was a conclusion to a proposition, which hardly suffices for a God who loves us.) This is not to say that understanding is incidental to faith; on the contrary, understanding aids and supports faith because understanding aids and supports the human person.

Thus another model for doing theology, one that might be more applicable to people today, is to begin in Jesus and work towards the understanding of God. Then one can continue from Jesus and God to what this faith implies for us. This is the process we will follow. Our first section began with Jesus, this section continues with the relation of Jesus to God. Our third section will explore the relationship between us, Jesus and God. If we summarized the content of theology, the entire theological enterprise is the explanation of these three relationships.

Understanding how God deals with humanity is difficult. We are not God. Nor do we set the parameters. The disciple is one who follows God's activity, and thus we follow God's ways with our understanding. In a sense, we are like Monday morning quarterbacks who see the game after it has been played. We reflect on God's actions, anticipate God's workings, participate in the activity, but cannot force God to be there nor determine the manner of his presence. One might say lightly that this indeterminacy of God has always foiled the best theological systems, and has contributed to the frustration of every theologian who has ever tried to locate God finally. God always reminds us that we do not contain him, we do not limit his ways. God is God. Sooner or later we are brought to this mystery. We yield finally to it, and wonder in awe.

Degrees of religious consciousness

Jesus told us that God wishes the salvation of all people. God loves everyone, even the sinner. Thus God is related to all. We call this relationship grace, which simply means God's self communicated to us. Grace creates a religious awareness whereby we can know and experience God through many manifestations. Sometimes grace is experienced as love, wonder, forgiveness, beauty, power, joy, gratitude, etc. Some call it an experience of the holy; others refer to it as the ultimate ground of being; still others as an openness to the wholly "Other" or "More" in life.

On the most basic level of consciousness, people everywhere, and throughout their lives, are open to this revelation of God.

There is a generally possessed religious consciousness that emerges from our humanity.

Beyond general consciousness lies a more explicit identification of this force by the name of "God." This specific consciousness of God we call theocentric. Throughout our human history, many peoples have specified the experience of the holy and called it by name. As humans, we express our understanding of God in the most important symbol reality that we know, that of our own humanity. Whether one calls God Yahweh, Allah, Brahman or one of the many other names, the identification is anthropomorphic. God is understood as caring, protecting, nurturing, providing for people. God acts like a person. Often God is seen with masculine characteristics of power, strength, and prowess, perhaps because of his size and stature. But feminine characteristics are always present as well in the gentleness, receptivity, patience, and compassion God invariably shows us. In the case of God, the qualities are infinitely greater and more extensive than they are in human expression. Thus God is all-knowing, all-powerful, all-present. Be that as it may, the revelation of God can only be communicated in terms that we can understand, in human metaphors and human experiences. That God resembles many of our heart's aspirations and dreams is a good thing. Instead of being afraid, humanity desires to befriend this God. We acknowledge our dependence and break out in worship. In so doing, we ourselves are exalted and befriended. Without hesitation, we say that we do know God and his ways.

Every religion claims some type of revelation. In Christianity, we understand the revelation of God to have been manifested in Jesus, who was of God. For Christians, an added explicitation of God exists. This is not of our making, it is God through Jesus. Therefore, our faith is Christocentric. Jesus shows us the Father and tells us how we can relate to God. The experience of believers verifies this relationship over and over again. God's power, life, and spirit are present to the believer, a unique human person with strengths and weaknesses, in discipleship.

In summary, God can be understood in three degrees of consciousness: religious, theocentric, and christocentric. Like concentric rings, they surround the same core. Why some are called into discipleship with Jesus and others are not remains a mystery. But there is also the mystery of being born into a particular family. All we know is that we must follow the truth as the Lord has given it to us, not excluding anyone from participation. We are sent on a mission to tell the entire world the good news of God's love and salvation for all. Yet the whole truth of God's ways is not clear to us. Nor do we understand his plan other than in the most general sense. We simply know that we must live this truth both for our sake and that of others.

Theology continually gropes to understand the workings of God. More reflection is needed, especially from other cultures and beliefs. Dialogue among world religions will prove to be of great benefit in the future—not with a view to converting people to Christianity, but rather to serve other people in their own conversion to God. Through this dialogue the revelation of Jesus will be found true. This is God's way. Those who know God will come to know Jesus' revelation. For how could it be otherwise? It is the one same God. Likewise, we will come to know how God has dealt with other persons and communities of believers. Theology today stands on the threshhold of new perceptions and understandings of God and his ways. Instead of denying the truth of other religions, we seem to be learning to respect them and to listen for what we can learn of God. This process will not be completed overnight. It is one of theology's major tasks for the future.

The Economic and Immanent Trinity

Who is the God that Jesus reveals? The Scriptures never speak about Jesus as completely identified with God. Jesus is the son of God which indicates that there is a parent-child relationship. Jesus refers to God as "abba," a familiar, intimate term which means dad. Because the evangelists never changed this Aramaic word indicates that Jesus probably used it and that it was central to Jesus' faith.

Because the father and the son are not the same, theology is left with the task of explaining their relationship. But this is not all. In the Christian experience, there is the Spirit. The presence of God given in Jesus remains with us in the form of God's very life itself. The Spirit is the very life of both the Father and the Son. Thus the revelation of Jesus always turns upon the Christian theology of the trinity, the three-in-oneness of God.

It is the trinity itself that is fundamental to Christian experience, not the theological concepts we use to speak about it. Theology attempts to formulate an understanding that is faithful to our experience, but does not say that the formulation itself is sacred.

The model traditionally used to interpret the trinity has been two-fold: the economic trinity and the immanent trinity. Let us begin by explaining the purpose, presupposition, and problem of each.

The immanent trinity refers to the way God is in himself. It is highly conceptual because no one knows God in himself. The presupposition at work is simply that God is one. This unity of God comes from our faith experience--we are not dealing with three gods.

Taking the radical oneness of God as our starting point, the problem becomes how to explain the relatedness of Jesus and God. The answer first came in the distinctions the Greek philosophers drew between person and nature. God has one nature which is divine. Yet there are three persons in God: the first person is the father, the second is the son, and the third is the holy spirit. They are related yet distinct from each other. The second person, the son, becomes flesh in Jesus. This model has dominated western Christian theology and is expressed most classically by Augustine (d. 420).

The economic trinity is the other model. "Economic" means "to manage the household." It refers to the way God managed salvation in history. The economic model is empirical: it interprets the way humanity experienced God through Jesus. It is historical as opposed to conceptual because it emphasizes the action of God in history. The presupposition at work in this model is God's threeness: the son revealed the father and the spirit dwells with us from the son. The father was present to us before Jesus: then Jesus showed us the father; finally the spirit was poured out upon us after Jesus' resurrection. God entered the world in three distinct sequential ways. The problem becomes acknowledging the unity of God without moving to a tri-theism. The answer lies in the tri-unity of God which corresponds to his nature. These are three modes or actions or manifestations of the same one God. This theology dominated the eastern church.

The models of the immanent and the economic trinity bear

an interesting resemblance to the problem of the humanity and divinity of Jesus. If one were to extend the high/low Christological model, one might say that we are dealing with a "high trinitology" and a "low trinitology." By this we mean that, like the high or descending Christology, the immanent trinity begins in *who* God is in himself and descends down to God's action in the world. Like low or ascending Christology, the economic trinity begins in God's *action* in the world through Jesus and ascends up toward who God is in himself. Just as low and high Christology are finally and inextricably two sides of the same coin, so too is the economic and immanent trinity really one. They are just two different starting points.

Now a further point needs to be made. Just as high Christology has dominated western theology, so has the immanent trinity. We have inherited an extremely conceptual understanding of the trinity which is removed from the historic salvation of the world in Jesus. The result is a God disconnected from salvation and seemingly independent of the world or us. We have a two-layered cake, then, with the supernatural above and the natural below. Theology today needs to return to the sources of trinitarian thought, namely Christology, and develop the economic trinity. For it is the economic trinity that relates God to the world and us to God. Because sin is the world, so too must be salvation. Moreover, the economic trinity makes the world and history the place of salvation, the place where God has established his Kingdom.

The corrective of the economic perspective is painfully needed. The trinitarian God in theology has become so complicated that Christians really do not think about it nor ask any questions about it with respect to their experiences. Yet the concept of trinity permeates the liturgical acts performed, the prayers said, and the faith experienced. Perhaps a return to faith experience and prayer (*lex orandi est lex credendi*=the law of praying is the law of believing) would provide a solid basis from which to begin. For example, when one prays, does one pray to the Father, the Son, or the Spirit? At times, the mystery of God is there—that is the Father. At other times, one prays to Jesus as access to the Godhead. At other times, one prays from the abiding presence characterized especially by peace and joy (the gifts of the Spirit). Either the trinity can be corroborated from the faith experience or else it is only a theological idea. The trinitarian relation of God is too important in our experience to let it go so lightly. Reflection upon our ordinary experience of God and formulations of these experiences are needed. Theology must be open to new insights into the trinity.

Some Suggestions

Any formulation of the trinity would do well to return to the Scriptures and Christology. From the scriptures, we know that Jesus is not the totality of the Godhead. He speaks about the Father. The Father remains the source of possibility. Jesus is the incarnation of the divinity into the world. About all we know is that this activity could not be done by the first or third person of the trinity. Jesus is the actualization of God in history. Jesus also speaks about the Spirit, who is neither Father nor Son. The Spirit comes only when Jesus returns to the Father in the resurrection-ascension. The Spirit is the spirit of the Father and the Son, sent to bring us closer to them. The Spirit is the source of unity.

In our liturgical prayers, we refer to the Father as the source of all; to the Son Jesus who came to save us and revealed the Father and our discipleship; and the Spirit who brings unity and dwells within us as God's very presence. The Father, Son, and Spirit are inseparable in reality, yet we can direct ourselves to the different activity and gift that each one brings us. The Christian knowledge of trinity is less explicit than it needs to be. We need new ways to reflect on our experience and present it as theology.

The trinity reveals important realities for us. If God is three-in-one, then God is, by nature, relational. God is social. The better model for the trinity might be that of a community. Then if God is related, we too share in this relation by being human. God would also be self-communicating; God does not give a thing but his very personal life itself. God is personal but extends even beyond what we can grasp as personal; he is transpersonal. The threeness of persons further indicates this transpersonal nature. The giving of one's person is what humans are called to do. In a word, this nature of giving and being is love. God is love in the deepest sense of person and living. This love has the characteristics of being related and relating others, involved and involving others, intertwined and intertwining others. As God loves so do we. The Kingdom of God can be summed up as love only because God is love. John said this well. The implication, that we are to be as God is, requires our loving others in this world to the fullest extent of love itself. It requires us to be related, involved, intertwined. To be a disciple is to live this love as Jesus showed us, in connectedness with God each day.

Another consideration that needs to be examined is the way this God initiates contact with us. God comes to us. In a way, God seems to be so in love with us that he cannot stay away. He desires us to share in his life. The presupposition is that God desires to communicate with us and be with us, not in any dependent way but in a mutually loving way. God chooses to make us important to his heart.

These are suggestions for developing the concept of trinity along the lines of contemporary theology. A more complete study needs to be done in order to encourage new insights. In the future, theology will be looking to new theologians who can contribute to this important area. It will be one of the most important areas of theological reflection in the decades to come.

Let us end this section with a reflection by the renowned theologian Karl Rahner, who says that there are two great mysteries in Christianity: the one is the incarnation, the other is the trinity. The relationship of God and humanity remains a profound mystery of love. To be complete in any theology, one must deal with these two mysteries which involve and intertwine us. Even though they remain irreducible mysteries that will never yield to final answers, nevertheless theology needs to articulate them as best it can. The mystery should not be the formulation by theology but the overwhelming love of a God who embraces us beyond our expectations. To remove mysterious answers in theology is always a correct step; to place oneself before the mystery of God is always good theology.

C. US: DISCIPLESHIP AND CHURCH

"Us" is an unusual title. It designates the human community, both past and present, with our common history and life. In traditional theology, one would expect the word "Church." Us includes Church, but goes wider. By using "us" we widen the concept of salvation to all people so the Church can serve God's

Kingdom wherever God indicates. Today, the Church is trying to understand its role in a new global way. The Church recognizes God's grace outside the Church as well as inside. The Kingdom of God includes the Church but it is not co-extensive with the Church. In other words, people can be saved without belonging to the Church as such. This outreach has lead theologians like Rahner to use such phrases as "anonymous Christian" to describe the extent of the Kingdom's boundaries. That particular phrase, however, has met substantial negative reaction because it limits the world to Christian categories. While the phrase is not as important as the reality, (even Rahner was willing to ditch it if a better one could be offered), nevertheless the Church must search for the right language in which to understand its relation to other peoples and God's kingdom.

Internal and External Identities

Another construct that might be helpful would be to differentiate between faith as internally discussed among believers and faith as externally discussed among non-believers. Two languages would result: one an internal language in which people shared the same faith experience and theology could begin from that point; the other an external language in which people did not share a common faith and theology had to speak in categories of common human experience. Since Vatican II the Church has in fact, through its theologies, embarked on both these courses. While they are not different faith paths in reality, and do not force a choice for one or the other, their language and style of communication are different. As an example, the council document *Gaudium et Spes* addresses an external audience consisting of "people of good will." In the document *Lumen Gentium*, the church fathers address an internal audience of believers. The former is known as a pastoral constitution and the latter a dogmatic constitution. This shifting of audiences has not been easy for those who believe that any distinction between internal and external is meaningless: either the Church speaks for everyone or everyone should listen to the Church. Sad to say, this position flies in the face of the Church's own directives. More importantly, it ignores the Church's role of service to the world.

The subject matter of people outside the Church has been discussed previously. God is present to them, saving them, and offering paths to follow him. We do not understand God's overall plan but we do know that salvation is part of it. Any thinking like "outside the Church there is no salvation" has no place in theologies of today. Theology is charged with understanding and articulating God's action so that we can follow it. When Peter followed the Spirit to Cornelius' house and recognized that God had visited the Gentiles without their entering into the old law, he offered them baptism without hesitation. This momentous event helped bring about an entirely new understanding of God's salvific grace, for the Gentiles as well as the Jews. Thus the Church entered into a new self-understanding of its role of evangelization in and throughout the world. The Church truly became a universal, a *catholic* Church.

Theology has talked about this area as missiology, i.e. "the study of the Church's mission." In fact, the Church is constituted for mission. It is a light on the mountain top, leaven in the dough, salt giving savor. Today missiology is a rapidly developing and increasingly extensive area of theology. For the first time, the young Churches are helping to determine the form of missionary efforts. This is an inculturated missiology or, as some theologians prefer to call it, an incarnational missiology. New developments in this area are expected to have significant contributions to theology.

In our day and age, we are witnessing what looks like the coming of a new Church: one that serves the global community. Vatican II inaugurated an openness to the world unprecedented except in the first century, when it was precipitated by the Cornelius event. Now the Church is journeying out into a cosmic age. A new self-understanding is being forged, but it is too early to know the specifics. Vatican II sketched it in the boldest and most sweeping terms, leaving the details to be filled in later.

Much work needs to be done on the Church's self-understanding as it relates to the world. The role of the Church involves nations, governments, races, classes, religions, non-believers, and, I believe most importantly, the global community of the future. "Community" will not automatically evolve; on the contrary, too many factors indicate that interglobal isolation will win out. However, if we are to live on this small planet, the Church's role and service will have to be discussed in a global context. And this will place significant demands on theology. The remainder of this section will deal with the internal dimension of Us, specifically, the believers. We call ourselves "Church." The etymology of Church is " a people assembled and assembling in the Lord." The emphasis is upon people. Throughout history, the Church has used many metaphors to explain its identity. The three main metaphors are "body of Christ," "temple of the holy Spirit," and "people of God." Many other possibilities exist as well. The basic relationship remains: a people called by God into a relationship with God and sent out on a mission. Our image of journey has expressed this. However, the Church remains a complex reality operating on many levels. One of the most helpful theological constructs has been to examine the Church in terms of basic relationships which form various models. The theologian Avery Dulles has been the principal articulator of this construct.

Models of the Church

Dulles began with five models of the Church and, some years later, added a sixth. The first five depict the Church as: institution; community; sacrament; herald or proclaimer; and servant. These five have been in the Church from the beginning. Dulles originally thought that sacrament might serve to unite the other four models. Because sacrament was used in Vatican II to describe the Church in the modern world, and because it encompassed the other models in their visible and invisible dimensions, it seemed appropriate. Most important, the Church as sacrament mediated the tension between the Church as institution and the Church as community.

However, a few years later, Dulles presented a sixth model: the Church as community of disciples. Rather than sacrament, it was discipleship which best summarized and held together the other models. Discipleship emphasizes the mission aspect of herald and servant models. It is founded on the earliest understanding of what it means to believe in Jesus, and it best describes his earliest followers. The Church as disciple suggests people on a journey, people with a relationship to God and a mission in the world. Anyone called to follow Jesus becomes a disciple and forms the people of God in the same faith. It is equally important for disciples to nurture their faith (internal) and to proclaim it in service (external). The discipleship model is in ascendency throughout contemporary theology; and the future will find it an increasingly important concept.

Just because community of disciples lays claim as an overarching model does not mean the other five are done away with. For example, the Church as institution is undergoing major stresses in the world today. The tensions between power and authority, obedience and freedom, traditional and new practices, personal and official charisms (e.g., prophecy versus administration)...are apparent in our life today. The Church is timebound, situated in history; it uses the best methods it can find. But better forms of communication, organization, decisionmaking, and responsibility continue to appear. For example, when no one was trained to help administer the sacraments, the priest did it all. But now with many people capable of administering the sacraments and a simultaneous shortage of priests, Eucharistic ministers and deacons can help serve the community. Because the lives of people change, so does the Church. Because we are a people, institutions will always be with us and so will the tensions they create. While institutions seek to deepen faith, we do not place any institution above Jesus. All institutional concerns are subordinate to serving the Lord in discipleship. For the sake of everyone, order and responsibility must be part of the life of believers; that the order and responsibility serve the Lord is our challenge. If our eyes remain on the Lord and each other, institutions will be a gracious gift that allow us to serve others better than we could alone. Institutionalizing can be a grace from God.

The tensions of institution are often practical ones which affect people's lives. Theology serves these practical decisions by providing and provoking the understanding behind them in relation to faith. Of themselves, decisions may or may not be of the gospel. Often decisions are prudential judgments about how we should proceed from here as a community. Any decision has to be interpreted for its particular circumstances. Differences in culture make the best way to live out a particular decision a choice which must be entrusted to the wisdom of the local communities, with an eye on its universal responsibility and accountability. If we all keep discipleship to the Lord uppermost and seek the Lord in one another, then institutionalization will work. But these efforts will always remain sticky and ambiguous. Tensions between individual and institutional, local and universal will remain. While many institutional decisions are not theological per se, theology must raise the broader questions of the relation of the Church as institution to discipleship. Seeking correct relationships in every part of our lives is good theology.

As with institution, so too will theology deal with the other four models of community, sacrament, herald, and servant. They comprise an area called ecclesiology, i.e., "study of the Church." One can see that ecclesiology extends in many directions and encompasses the life of the believer and his or her relations to all people. The line between internal and external becomes blurred, as do the boundaries of each of the models. The Church is greater than various models can reflect. It overflows all categories.

The Church is comprised of the disciples of the Lord, each with different gifts and charisms, but all given the very same Spirit of Jesus and the Father. The Spirit constitutes the unifying and vivifying source of the Church. To this extent the Church is divinely founded. At the same time, God invites us to help build his Kingdom. Although we do not make the Kingdom from our own resources, we do help bring it about by our participation. Even as people can be saved without knowing about Jesus or the Church, so too can they participate in the bringing of the Kingdom. Those who feed the hungry, clothe the naked, and do what the Spirit directs, create God's Kingdom. Their actions are the actions of God. As Church we know God's revelation and so encourage others to find him. We serve both God and humanity by the truth of our lives. We believe that God will call all people in his own way, and we pray that we can recognize God's spirit at work in the world. By participating in the Kingdom ourselves we extend our faith as an invitation for others to "come and see" the Lord in discipleship.

Although the Church is divinely founded upon the Spirit, the Church never gives up its human face. God does not take away our humanity, our frailty, our weaknesses, our vulnerabilities. Neither can we draw a clear line between divine and human elements in the Church; they are inextricably one. To this extent the Church is a sacrament—both human and divine, visible and invisible—of God's enduring love in the world. The Church is the visible gift of Jesus through the Spirit: the Father is found and the Kingdom arrives. The Church is like leaven in the dough of human history, a light of promise and fulfillment to shine for all people, a salt which brings the taste of the real Kingdom. Through human persons united by the same Spirit, the Church lives. Still searching, seeking, following, journeying, looking for the Lord in our history, meeting him and being called to meet him elsewhere, so the Church lives.

Sacraments

When the Church finds the Lord, it celebrates. These celebrations constitute the sacraments internal to the Church: baptism, confirmation, reconciliation, eucharist, anointing of the sick, matrimony, and holy orders of ministry. When faith is found, baptism occurs and is confirmed in the Spirit. When sinners find the Lord, reconciliation takes place in the community. When lives change for the Church, matrimony and holy orders are celebrated. We celebrate God's salvation even in sickness and death. And for the daily bread which sustains us, eucharist is celebrated. Eucharist ("thanksgiving") is the central sacrament in the Church's life: we celebrate God's word, the gift of his grace in Jesus, and the Spirit in community. Eucharist creates a regular rhythm of support and celebration for the community of disciples called Church.

Each of the sacraments is a communal act, symbolic in form, and salvific in action. Because sacraments are communal, they belong to the entire people as manifestations of God's life within the Church. The sacraments teach us to become more attentive to the Lord in our lives. By his word, his bread, and his people, we come to know the Lord more intimately and our friendship with him is deepened. Meanwhile the community continually offers new encouragement, helping us recognize the Spirit in our lives, and calling us to renew our commitment in discipleship.

The sacraments form an area of theology: faith in action. Here we cannot remain on the theoretical, abstract level; sacraments are the actions of disciples. They are the special moments of Christian life that build the faith of God's disciples. The way life and theology come together in sacraments needs continual exploration. The symbolic or sacramental side of each action comes from a history rooted in faith, extends our belief into community, and calls us to respond to God in our lives again. While sacraments belong to the believing community, their importance goes further. The sacraments focus the disciple for living in the world and coming to recognize the Lord in every facet of life. They also sustain us in that journey. Sacraments act like provisions in our knapsack as we journey in discipleship. We do not take any extra shoes or pants or money; we take the Lord's presence in ourselves and in our community, celebrating it when we can, then continuing our journey. The sacraments are not ends in themselves, therefore, but gifts for our journey. They belong to the Church.

As lived faith internally celebrated by the community of disciples, sacraments are an important area of theological reflection. As the symbolic actions of disciples, sacraments are often the particular ways people enter into a knowledge of and relationship with God. Sacraments are theologies in action. Vatican II called for a renewed understanding of the importance and meaning of the sacraments, reminding us that they were rich, often untapped resources for people in the modern world. Many developments in sacramental theology have occurred since then, and more are on the horizon. Slowly the richness of these gifts to us is becoming more apparent, and their role in our lives more important.

Spirituality and Prayer

Two final areas that contribute to doctrinal theology are spirituality and prayer. Understanding comes from the consequences of our individually committed actions that need to be related within communal responsibilities. Spirituality and prayer are two important contributors to a deep and integrated faith in thought and action. While a complete discussion of these areas is not the purpose of this study, we will attempt a brief and important explanation of how they relate to discipleship as Church.

The way a disciple lives out his or her life, constantly pulling aspects of faith into the light, making commitments and living in fidelity to them, and growing in the journey of the Lord—this is Christian spirituality. It is all the life choices that flow from one's faith commitment. One could say that Jesus died for his spirituality, meaning the rich and deeply personal relationship with the Father that involved Jesus in solidarity with all humanity. We do not have the same spirituality as Jesus but we do possess his gift of the Holy Spirit. Each of us is different and possesses different gifts or charisms. Each integrates, structures, and expresses his or her talents in a different way. Sometimes a spirituality is shared, as are the Franciscan, Dominican, or Jesuit spiritualities. These have been approved by the Church as truly rendering the one great spirituality of faith: discipleship. These various spiritualities are based on a few Christian gifts which are then lived out in a way beyond the normal demands of Christian faith. For example, not everyone is expected to live with vows of poverty, chastity, and obedience. Those who do have freely chosen this as the best way to commit their gifts to a life of faith. Understanding comes from these life commitments and provides a fertile field for systematic reflection.

Spirituality must be tested to see if it presents the gospel clearly, without distorting or falsifying it. This is one service that theology offers. By seeking to understand why we act in this or that way, measuring it against the gospel and the community of faith we can better judge the authenticity of our spirituality. There is always the danger that a spirituality will degenerate into cult or brain-washing. The gospel gives freedom, not slavery.

The last two decades have seen tremendous ground swells in spirituality. Before this time, it belonged to the ascetical theology which came at the end of theological training. But the drive to unify theology with life resisted this abstraction and re-ordered theology to life practices. Spirituality, the lived faith experience which comes from the core of the individual and the community, called upon theology for new understandings. At the same time, people found in spirituality a practical flow for their formal faith commitments. Once it was mainly the religious orders who performed, preserved and fostered spirituality but today people of all vocations are embracing it in many explicit forms. Coming as it does from the lived faith experience, spirituality will prove a rich resource in the future of theology.

Along with spirituality, much attention has been given to prayer. Both communally and individually, prayer connects us with God, making it possible for us to know and understand him. At times theology turns to prayer to verify its findings. At other times, prayer turns to theology to measure its authenticity. When prayer becomes a source of decision, it is called discernment. The disciple desires to know God's will even as Jesus did. So in imitation of Jesus, the disciple turns to prayer. Prayer is the act of relating to God by lifting up one's awareness to him. In prayer, a conversation goes on in which communication with God is the goal. We pray not because we are Christians but because we are human. Prayer emerges from the heart, almost of its own accord. We turn to God when a baby is sick, when we are in trouble, when our hearts overflow with suffering or joy. We seem not to be able to help it. That we are truly relational persons needs no explanation at these times.

Theology serves the experience of prayer, relates it to the entire gospel message, and measures its relationship to the faith experience of the community and tradition. Prayer has always been a source for doing theology: consider the great mystics Theresa of Avila and John of the Cross. With greater attention to prayer and the increased interest in spirituality, theology stands to be better and stronger, provided it remains in close contact with these lived experiences.

Christian discipleship celebrates its life in sacrament and worship, seeks God in the committed action of spirituality and continues an ongoing relationship with God in prayer. These are practices of our faith, which flow into faith and out of faith, and we refer to them as practical theology. They include many areas of decision-making, life values and morality, the full scope of which is beyond this series.

Theology derives its task from faith, and judgements about the practice of faith are important sources for theology. The model is thus: active faith (action) seeking understanding (theology) which sends its findings back to decision and action. Practical theology has developed extensively since Vatican II, and with it theoretical constructs. The cycle of action, reflection, and action has ordered theological concerns and opened them to lived experience and renewed interpretations. In the final analysis, theology belongs to the community of disciples and serves that community by deepening its understanding of Jesus' invitation to follow him in a journey with the Spirit to the Father. This invitation involves commitment and responsibility to grow in our relationship of love with God and one another. Each of us will do this in a different way depending upon our charisms but, if our relationships and actions are of the Lord, we will always grow together in the same Spirit.

3

Theology and Its Tools

In this last section, we will examine theology's relation to language, texts, and culture. They are the conversation partners through which theology develops in its own thought. In our first section, we examined theological anthropology, which forms the foundation for subsequent theological investigation. In our second section, we examined the basic relationships between Jesus, God, and us. Each of these three terms begins in a content of its own and extends outward to say something about the other two concepts. Finally, we will consider how the content of theology comes down to us through language, texts and tradition. These are important components of theology; like conversation partners, they remind theology how it developed, and how much it continues to depend on them.

A study of language and texts can be bland and abstract—but it need not be. Think how impoverished we would be without language. No books, no symbols, no stories... Language and texts are filled with the life blood of human experience; filled with human understanding and imagination. Our challenge in theology is to return language and texts to the human base and the study of human communication they provide for us. As we have done throughout this book, we will enter the discussion from the viewpoint of theological anthropology. Hopefully, this examination will reveal more about these important conversation partners.

1. Theology and Language

Theology depends on language. Words are like ships that transport ideas, meaning, emotions, concerns, and loves from one person to another. The action unites the sender with the receiver. The word "communicate" means "to make common." We communicate with one another through language, sometimes spoken, at other times written. While language can be non-verbal (e.g., gestures, symbols) as well as verbal (speech or writing), we will concentrate here on verbal language. (In both cases language belongs to a people, is one of their strongest forms of identity, and is both a social act and an intensely individual act.)

When theology, which is "God-talk," speaks about God whom we have never seen, it cannot simply point to God and say "See for yourself." God remains hidden. Everything we say about God is a metaphor. God "is like" this, we say, appealing to what we know as humans to express what goes beyond the limits of our language. For example, when we talk about where God is, we point beyond the fluffy white clouds and say "heaven." When we talk about who God is, we know God is strong and provides for us, so we say "father." When we speak about God's presence with us, we call God the "Holy Spirit that dwells among us." We use a series of familiar images to say something quite new. Because God is not to be mistaken for our metaphors, he remains known and unknown at once. We are attempting to describe the indescribable and explain the mysterious. Our language will always be incomplete, limited, and humanly conditioned. We acknowledge these constraints—yet continually strain to go beyond them. We do this every time we tell someone that we love them! That language both limits us and sets us free is no surprise. But we often forget that the limits of language affect theology and all other discourse about God.

A few examples may help to concretize a rather abstract topic. When I speak with another person, I intend many types of language-humor, irony, narration or story... I can usually see whether my listener understands what I am saying by his or her response. If no one sees the humor of what is said, then the communication is poor. If I tell an important story about myself which is deeply painful and people respond by breaking out in sudden laughter, I feel confused, angry, and betrayed. By others' gestures, smiles, eyes, nods, body language, etc., I see whether or not communication is taking place. When someone not only hears my story but responds with understanding, communication has occurred. When someone listens and then speaks to the other, a conversation has begun. Points are clarified, more understanding is asked for, similar experiences are shared. Two people are meeting and knowing each other; a friendship develops.

Human persons are symbols themselves; we are not transparent. We come to know another only if that other chooses to reveal his or her self. We are self-revelatory people who must break the silence. In this way we mirror God who does the same to us. What we call revelation is simply communication with God. As social beings, we desire to be known and to know others. The extent of how many can know me or how many I can know seems to vary from person to person. Some can have many close friends while others need only a few. But in every case, persons must break the silence of their lives and reveal themselves by "making something common," i.e., communicating.

Listening is not an easy act. It requires hearing accurately what is said, not layering the other's words with my prejudiced ideas or feelings. It requires withholding judgment, getting into both the mind and feeling of the other, and *understanding*.

If a person speaks to me in Chinese and I do not understand the language, no matter how well the other describes his or her feelings, I will not understand. A common set of words (vocabulary), the order and relationships between them (grammar) and their meanings (semantics) must all be present if communication is to occur. Of course these are non-verbal forms of communication—gestures, facial movements, intonation, loudness or softness—which aid the verbal effort. Through all these expressions communication occurs. It is our skill at using them that makes us good communicators.

In writing, a person does not have this wide range of expression. Moreover, writing does not allow one to be physically present. Hence the burden of communication rests totally on the written word. The options that a reader can choose must be anticipated and limited, so the reader will find the meaning the author intended. It is like leading a person through a maze of ideas to a specific, predetermined destination. In writing one sees the words of another but does not hear the voice. The intonation and emphasis usually provided by speech must somehow be included in the written word. The words must be heard. Thus the reader becomes the voice. This transfer of interpretive powers explains why the written word needs to be understood in a different way than speech. The two forms of communication are both language communication, but they are very different in form.

Theology shares in both the oral and written forms of communication. In the classroom or lecture halls, theology is usually oral. Because the audience can hear and respond, some theologians prefer this type of communication. But as a discipline, theology rests primarily on the written word for classification and transmission. People from all over the world can enter into this written conversation. (Hence languages remain an important tool for theologians.)

Universal dialogue allows for a richer mix of theological thoughts and insights. This universal dialogue takes place on the pages of all the discipline's books and journals. Each specialty (e.g., biblical, doctrinal, moral, spirituality) uses a slightly different vocabulary. With the increasing variety of visual and voice communication media (videotapes, cassette tapes, etc.) there will no doubt be greater dissemination of theological communication. Television and radio now offer universal dissemination that was unheard of just a few years ago. The power of these media challenges theology to make use of their form of communication.

While writing remains the language of the specialists among themselves, and one must read those theologians to understand the field, theirs is not necessarily the language of the layperson. It is arguable whether writing is the preferred communication form of the masses. Newspapers and magazines disseminate information but the oral form remains our most basic communication. People talk about articles, stories, events. Television has conditioned people to see and hear news. Deep down in our humanity, we prefer the oral and visual forms of communication. Modern technology has made the variety of communication forms accessible and instantaneous. Theology does not have to wait for an information explosion. The explosion has already happened. Theology must catch up.

Some of the forms used to communicate theology have a long history through which the conversation has become very sophisticated. For example, when the Vatican issues a dogmatic constitution it does so in a particular way. The format resembles that of a diplomatic statement, and the style is full of nuances. To understand a conciliar or papal document we must be familiar with this format, which strikes many people as unusual and antiquarian, difficult to read and comprehend. The truth is that most people do not read conciliar documents. Hence their communicative power is limited. The Vatican's challenge is to remain universally responsible to many cultures. It has no special language and format that pleases everyone. In former times, even if the format was unpopular, the content could at least be written in latin, the universal language of the Church. Today there is no universal language and the format of most ecclesial documents remains the traditional one. But rather than discount this form of communication because it is difficult, we must take it seriously because of its source. Theology must work to keep the lines of communication flowing in both directions. It would also seem that a variety of communications at different levels would be welcome; and, indeed, some of the recent U.S. bishops' pastoral letters have been steps in that direction. Undoubtedly the future will see even more forms of communication in use.

No matter what form the message takes, differences in language and communication bring their own problems. There are no easy solutions. Therefore, every Church document requires interpretation and should not be presumed to apply literally across different cultures and languages. In fact, some bishops' pastorals explicitly do *not* apply uniformly. That problems in interpretation exist should not surprise anyone. Throughout the United States each year, we spend billions of dollars and countless number of hours in law courts arguing over the interpretation of words. The Supreme Court routinely makes final determinations of the law for the land interpreting the intended meaning of one word.

Likewise, understanding theological statements from the past is not easy. Cultural and linguistic differences, as well as changes in historical consciousness, make correct communication difficult. For instance, one cannot read a contemporary understanding of "person" back into the important conciliar documents of Ephesus (431) or Chalcedon (451) without grossly misunderstanding them. If we speak of the person and nature of Jesus and the Trinity in the 5th century categories and simply attach 20th century meanings, we will communicate almost the exact opposite of what was originally intended. Simple repetition of historical categories or words distorts them. Texts are the product of a human time and place and are not transparently self-explanatory. Just as modern communication of every sort requires hard work, so do texts of the past. Theology takes all communication seriously—especially communication from the past. Theology desires never to be mired in tradition nor simply awash in the present; it searches for God's wisdom and truth everywhere.

One final point needs to be made. Even as theology continually strives for better communication of the experience of God, it does so from a moving viewpoint. No Archimedian stillpoint outside human living exists. Theology does not determine who God is; only God does that. Like a disciple, theology listens to God and tries to understand: faith seeks understanding. Also like a disciple, theology keeps a humble attitude. Theology searches, probes, teases out, lures, gathers up, explains, and explores the frontiers of human relationships with God. As soon as theology thinks it has everything explained, God breaks it all open again. Theology's point of view moves with the active presence of God, as the disciple moves on his or her journey. Because it is dynamic, theology is reformable, approximate, disclosive, pointing. It serves to bring others to the ineffable experience of God, instead of offering itself as a substitute for the experience. Theology does not seek to be worshipped or glorified. It serves a Christian community on behalf of the entire world, in response to God's call to proclaim the good news. As people respond through many different styles of discipleship, so too does theology express the differences in method and viewpoint. And just as no one form of discipleship is complete or superior, no one theology will suffice to express the rich diversity of God's dealings with us.

Language will always remain a challenge because human

persons change. We continually communicate with one another our new realizations of what and who is most important. Better understanding of language and communication is essential to theology; one need not fear it. A more thorough understanding of language will free us of our ignorance and bring us to a purified awareness of the real mystery of God. As said before, the real mystery of God is not contained in the unknown answers to our questions; but in God's unlimited embrace and love of humanity. To say that God is mystery is to say that God is a never-ending adventure in loving.

2. Theology and Texts

Language and communication come in many forms, not all of which have the same priority or importance. From the many written and verbal sources, a theological conversation begins. Theology dialogues with many partners. The most pressing dialogue partner is the immediate circumstances of our lives. The suffering of humankind, the pain of alienation, the struggle to be good, and the social dependence upon life-giving decisions fashion the immediate and concrete circumstances from which theology emerges. When theology springs from present needs, it is hot, alive, and pressing. It bristles and crackles with urgent everyday needs. Yet, not all questions of theology come from immediacies. Some questions are asked by others through a 2000 year tradition. A text, person, or event which has shaped the Christian faith becomes part of our past and, in a sense judges whatever is done today. Hence theology also dialogues with the rich tradition of the past. When it does, one might expect the conversation to be cold, barely alive, and irrevelant. But this assumption is not true. The study of biblical, patristic, medieval, reformation, modern, and contemporary theology provides a larger faith perspective, offers options long forgotten, suggests new possibilities, and frees people to make creative responses. The past offers possibilities beyond the immediacies of the present; it increases our options and stimulates our imaginations. Thus the past bears directly upon the present, and can contribute to a true and solid response to immediacies. An understanding of how theology dialogues with the past will help us understand the nature of theology.

The Canon of Scripture

One source for doing theology is the collection of written works about our faith. We shall begin with the most important: the New Testament. Comprised of a collection of 27 books, not all of them equally important or significant, the new Testament represents the earliest witness to the Christian faith. Because this witness embodies the earliest Christian experiences, even eye-witness accounts, it stands above any work designated as "theology." We call it revelation. "Revelation" means that God shows us something about our life and his role in it. In the New Testament, Jesus reveals to us the Father and the meaning of discipleship. Because it contains our earliest witness, Scripture remains special to our faith experience today.

The collection of four gospels, epistles (letters), Acts of the Apostles, and Book of Revelation (Apocalypse) is called a "canon" of Scripture. "Canon" comes from the word "cane," a reed that might grow in a marsh. A cane or reed stands straight and, if cut to an exact length, can easily become a measuring stick. Hence a canon means a norm or standard by which something is measured. The 27 books of the New Testament form a canon which measures Christian experience. Each diverse culture and every generation receives the authentic Christian experience as it has come from the earliest communities. The canon, as we know it, began to form in the second century because the heretic Marcion rejected the entire Old Testament and abbreviated New Testament books. By the year 200 a definition of an orthodox canon appeared which, with minor exceptions, was generally accepted until the Reformation era.

As a measuring device, the canon is finished. No more books will be added. In this sense the canon of scripture is closed. But four additional statements need to be made. First, although the canon is closed, this does not imply that no other manuscripts of tremendous importance will be unearthed.

The second point follows from the first and is more important. The canon of scripture is not intended to act as a closed door that denies the importance or significance of other works. In fact, other works can often be more helpful to faith than the New Testament canon. For example, the *Imitation of Christ* might be more meaningful to me than any other book. (We might remember that Catholics rarely read the New Testament even though they listened to parts of it at worship services.) So we need to find some way of understanding the importance of the canon of the New Testament relative to other written works. Even as we say this, however, we must remember that the Scriptures go beyond being written documents to be read; they were intended to be heard, to be proclaimed in the assembly; to open the heart of the believer.

Third, because the canon is a norm, it must be applied. Even when the canon was being gathered together in the second century, the Christian community had already experienced the need to draw life from the scriptures for their own living situation. With persecutions from Rome breaking out sporadically, new cities and territories becoming Christian, and the gradual ethnic change from a Jewish to Greco-Roman culture, the Christians knew that they had to use the gospel to guide their lives. Christians today know this same need. The canon of Scripture does not address impending nuclear devastation, democratic governments, computers, television, telephones, and automobiles. This is the twentieth century context. But the writers of the Scriptures did know about salvation, and they testified to it. While we cannot step out of our twentieth century context, we can measure it by the New Testament. When Christians read or hear the Scriptures today, they can say "This is our experience." To recognize one's own faith in the New Testament canon is to verify the authenticity of the canon and say again that it stands both as a special gift of God's revelation and a measure of our experience today.

Fourth, our faith is not dependent upon the canon. We possess the Holy Spirit who is God's own spirit within us. Thus, when we recognize the same faith in our lives and in the canon, it is this Spirit that we recognize. The canon is a gift of the Spirit and the earliest communities of faith from which every Christian benefits.

Let us come at this point in another way. What if there was a world-wide catastrophe whereby all the books in the world were destroyed? Included in this loss would be all the copies of the

New Testament. What would we do? We would have our memories and oral tradition. We would begin to write down all that we remembered about Jesus, the stories we recalled, the experiences of the early followers, the meaning of the early Church in living community, Eucharist, and sacraments. We would ask other people to collect their memories of our faith experience, and we would gather this collective memory together. Then we would write it down to preserve, clarify, and disseminate it through the community. We would then judge what information was true, what we all agreed upon, what we judged extraneous, and what we considered important but of lesser significance. And if we were not sure, we might form a second set of writings. The reason why we would take such pains to gather this information comes from our need to preserve the authenticity of our faith. In fact we would be writing a second canon, only this time it would come 2000 years later and without direct personal contact with Jesus. Still, I have no doubt that the Holy Spirit would generate the same fidelity to the experience.

The purpose of imagining this scenario is to present the specialness of the New Testament canon and its function in our faith. The canon did not intend to end discussion of faith but to set the parameters for further discussion. Implicit within the notion of the canon itself is the idea that the context of faith changes both in place and in time, i.e., from culture to culture and down through history. Otherwise, if it did not recognize changes occurring, the Church would have no need to gather together the principal documents of the Christian faith and offer them to people. Any attempt to put the canon up on a pedestal as untouchable and untouching, as if Christian experience was totally finished and expounded for all times and places, is a misuse of the canon. For, as Jesus said, God is not a God of the dead but of the living. The God who dwells within us makes any and all measure possible. Neither God nor we live in the past, but from the past, in the present, and toward the future.

With regard to the Old Testament canon, the same principles hold. The one difference with the Old Testament canon is that we, as Christians, interpret it in light of our faith experience. Without the New Testament canon, the Old Testament canon would make no sense for Christians. Thus the New Testament canon forms the principle of interpretation for the Old Testament canon. In the order of importance to faith, the New Testament comes first and the Old Testament second. However, in the order of salvation history, we acknowledge our lineage and debt to the Jewish faith.

While the New Testament canon remains special, privileged, and central to our faith, it is not the final word. From the point of view of revelation, the Scriptures are a category unto themselves; and then we have all the other writings about faith. Theology examines both the scriptures and all of these other writings, even adding to them. Some type of theological construct might be in order to help us understand these writings. The theologian David Tracy has suggested the idea of the "classic." Because we are dealing with written texts of the Christian tradition, this analogy seems appropriate.

The Classic

In art and literature, the best example of a work that lasts is a classic. A "classic" is the best known expression of its particular content. When speaking about religion, a classic is the best expression of our faith life. It extends down through history, often transculturally, and successive generations reconfirm its relevance. The classic discloses the meaning of the faith experience in such a way that a person says, "This is important. This will make a difference!" The gospels, for example, are classics, and continually evoke this kind of response.

Classics also challenge the world-view of the reader. In a sense, the classic steps outside the boundaries of space and time to meet the believer and challenge his or her belief. This timeless quality is one mark of a classic, and the ability to challenge one's world-view is another. But the most important characteristic of a classic is that it discloses the universal truth underlying individual experience. Thus a classic's purpose is not informational but transformational. It brings us into the grasp of holy mystery which changes us. In a back-and-forth dialogue the classic challenges the believer to become converted. And, as a statement of truth, it remains the possession of all people.

Classics are not made in heaven. They undergo a process before they are raised to the status of classics. First, certain individuals find them compelling, and others agree. Then, as time passes other generations agree, and other believers in diverse cultures confirm it, and so on down through the ages.

Classics require interpretation. They reveal reality and truth as well as seal it in a form. Their power and authority come not from simple repetition but from their ability to re-present faith, to bring its truth into the present moment. We enter into the spaces described by the classic and find that they contain the truth of our lives. Simple repetition of the gospel of Mark, for example, will not render the disclosive power of Mark to another generation. Only religious experience on the individual's part will allow him or her to understand what Mark meant. Titles such as the Son of Man, Messiah, or Son of David may not be transparent to subsequent generations. The text must be opened up before it can disclose itself.

Theologians are interpreters of the classics. They open up the text to allow its disclosive power to enter into the lives of others. They allow re-presentation to occur by readying the believer and providing understanding of the text. They also remind the reader that, as disclosive and appealing, classic form is not the truth itself.

Classics can be divided into two groups: major classics and minor classics. The difference rests in the scope, comprehensiveness, and completeness of the classic. For example, the gospels remain major classics while Paul's letter to Timothy is a minor classic, even though canonical. The *Confessions* of Augustine are a major classic; his sermons are not. A few other classics are the *Summa Theologica* of Thomas Aquinas, the *Imitation of Christ* by Thomas a Kempis; and Theresa of Avila's *Interior Castle*.

The process of becoming a classic is long and exacting, and many works fall by the wayside. Then ones that fail may be refreshing but lack the transformative powers. Sometimes the work seems to bring together the faith experience of the moment but falls short when judged by time. For example, early in one's life a work becomes significant. In older age, one evaluates the timeless message of that work differently, and sees it not as timeless but as extremely important at one time in life. Such works can be descriptively designated as period pieces or heirlooms.

Heirlooms are those texts that we hold precious even though their disclosive power does not match that of a classic. Many of the letters of the Fathers of the Church, such as those of Irenaeus, Tertullian, Dionysius, and Athanasius fall into this category. While they have an enduring quality and remain precious to the believing family of Christians, they lack the great staying power of a classic. Like heirlooms, their expressions are important and valuable, and even increase in value when they are passed down from generation to generation—but they do not possess the rich quality of a treasure, as a classic does.

A period piece is a text that spoke to its period but failed to last. It too can be refreshing but not transformative. A period piece may have been full of insights for a specific community, but it failed to extend beyond the borders of their experience to other times and places. Unlike heirlooms, which contain a general importance which can be passed down in time by the believing community, period pieces are locked up in time. Their disclosive power is enclosed in the time that nurtured them. To understand them requires a great deal of work and a return to the period of their significance. Many works at or after the time of the Reformation (1517) belong to the difficulties of that time. While the timely catechism of Peter Canisius was extremely important for his world, it is weighed down by the polemics of that time and thus fails to reach the stature of a classic.

Similarly, many of the works that were acknowledged as outstanding before the Vatican II council are now seen in another light. These works were culturally conditioned and unable to extricate their disclosive power from the time and place of its origin. Many of the works on Jesus were powerful and helpful at the time, but a return to Scripture and the addition of historical and literary criticism have contributed new insights, showing these works to be embedded in a particular cultural situation. When that situation changes, the works do not contain the disclosive power to cross the boundaries of time and place and emerge as classics. They remain disclosive only for their period.

This model of the classic concerns itself with texts but is not limited to texts. It could extend to any form of religious communication: an event, a symbol, a gesture, a person. The event of Jesus, the Eucharistic service, the person of Francis of Assisi, the sign of the cross, etc., are classics. The theologian re-presents and interprets these too. Our point of entrance was the text: although it has now lead us to a wider understanding of classic, the purpose of the theologian remains the same. The theologian serves theology by understanding and interpreting classics, offering new ones, judging others, and waiting for others to prove their worth. For the most part, theologians themselves write period pieces, some heirlooms, rarely a classic. But this stream of material enriches the faith, strives to present new forms, and stirs the waters to find still others. Classics are rare and always emerge from the nourishing waters of faith. To this extent, the flowing stream of water remains more important than the discovery of new classics. But once the classic occurs, it gushes forth fresh water forever into the stream of theology and the faith it serves.

Most theologians do not attain the stature of even contributing to minor classics. The community of theologians continually strives for explanations that provide understanding for faith today. It is not within the power of a theologian to make a classic. It remains for the people of later generations to judge. Writing a classic is not ordinarily the quest of a theologian. The theologian works to keep the stream of faith as deep and rich as possible. To do this, the theologian enters into conversation with a wide range of dialogue partners from the past and the present. Even then, the theologian remains open to other voices.

Conclusion:
Profile of a Theologian

Our study began with human anthropology as the context for theology. We found that the major building blocks of theology in the origin myth of Genesis are sin, salvation, and faith (Part I). Each building block supports additional concepts such as the Kingdom of God, grace, obedience, hope, and love. Then we saw that theological anthropology finds its key relationships in the understanding of Jesus, God, and us (Part II). Theology revolves around our understanding of these three topics, taken both individually and together. Finally, we identified the sources for our understanding of these topics and relationships, which take the form of language and texts (Part III). It seems only fitting to end where we began: with the human person.

We will speak of a specific human person: you, the reader. What happens to you when you study theology? While this is impossible to determine ahead of time, we can see what happens to others. The conclusion of our study will take the form of a reflection about being a theologian. Although this description does not pretend to be complete or normative in any sense, it does purport to be a common profile. The contention is that if one enters into the study and doing of theology, then one can expect to find changes occurring in one's self. One enters into the fundamental questions of life and the most basic commitments human persons make. One enters one's own conversion process. The profile of a theologian is a metaphor of what might happen to anyone. The following reflection seeks, first or all, to stimulate, evoke, and encourage each person in his or her pursuit of theology. Secondly, it indicates that one is never alone in doing theology—one does theology in a tradition and within a community of believers. Thirdly, each person's contribution to theology is most welcome and puts the richness of his or her faith experience at the disposal of others. As good theology, it always serves the Lord and others. Good theology is good ministry.

Profile of a Theologian

Above all, the theologian is a disciple. Luke gives us this image in his description of the life of Jesus as a journey. Beginning in Galilee to the north and stretching to Jerusalem in the south, this journey represents the personal following of the will of God. Geography is itself a metaphor for the journey every person makes in returning to the Father. Journey is the symbol of the life of a disciple. One not only learns but also follows the master wherever he goes. As the model of discipleship, Jesus obeyed the Father. Jesus leaned upon God with all his weight (the definition of faith) and he proclaimed the Kingdom of God. His faith took him to different towns, to the outcast and the marginal; in short, wherever the Spirit led. Wherever he went and to whomever he met, he showed both his love and that of the Father. Jesus showed his love in compassion, in forgiveness, in solidarity with the poor. And when people came to him, he told them to follow him. Those who did became disciples.

The profile of a theologian might best be glimpsed in Luke's culminating story of the two men on their way to Emmaus. On that Easter morning, they had left the other disciples and journeyed away from Jerusalem. Discouraged, confused, seeking answers, they talked. A stranger came up behind them and greeted them, asking what they were speaking about. They were shocked that the stranger did not know about Jesus' death in Jerusalem. And, they continued, women had just returned from the tomb saying that his body had disappeared. They had believed in Jesus but they did not understand.

As they walked, the stranger began to interpret the scriptural text about how the son of man would have to suffer and so enter into glory. Things began to make sense; the interpretation became clearer. Unwilling to let the stranger go, they asked him to stay for dinner. While at dinner, they recognized him "in the breaking of the bread." Then he disappeared. They ran back to their friends in Jerusalem to tell them what happened and how their hearts had burned with the truth that came with understanding.

Theologians' hearts have not stopped burning since. Nor have they kept their understandings quiet. The truth seeks to reveal itself and, while no theologian claims to hold the whole truth, each theologian renders it the best way he or she can. Jesus continues to disappear just as he did for the two disciples. Theologians seek to recognize his presence wherever and whenever he appears. It is not insignificant that the two disciples found Jesus in "the breaking of the bread", a common reference to the Eucharistic liturgy. Often the theologian finds God—or rather God finds the theologian—in ordinary events and symbols. The theologian tries to understand and articulate the meaning of the relationship.

The journey requires the entire person and asks for a complete conversion: intellectual, affective, moral, and religious. Along the way, the theologian offers his or her understanding of this journey to others. As the two disciples on the way to Emmaus show us, the life and work of a theologian remain always that of a disciple on a journey.

The theologian freely chooses, as a disciple, to enter the discipline of theology. He or she then studies, learns the tradition, the methods, the content, the classics, etc., in an attempt to become competent. Because theology depends upon a community of interpretation, a basic minimum of training is usually required. Although academic degrees do not measure faith, they do provide a measure of competency. On paper, degrees indicate a type of training and professional achievement. Some degrees are ecclesiastical degrees, conferred by a particular religious tradition, e.g., S.T.D. (Doctorate in Sacred Theology). Others are academic degrees conferred by universities, e.g., Ph.D. or M.A.. Each theologian has different strength: research, interpretation, communication, pastoral, systematizing, constructive, or practical skills. No one possesses all of them, yet every one of these skills is needed.

Behind the credential lies the whole process one went through to earn it. A degree does not tell us what challenges the person encountered, or what results he or she achieved in motivation, belief, life, and faith. The degree actually represents both a level of training achieved and a type of program undertaken. But it means little if the theologian has not begun the process of personal integration. In sum, a person is educated in theological skills and competency.

The journey, even through academic programs, is not always what one expects. In fact, one might advise the student to expect the unexpected. Challenges will come up from behind, as did the stranger at Emmaus.

I remember one example very vividly in my own program. I was doing a degree in historical theology, and the history of the popes, potentates, inquisition, crusades, schisms, and political decisions had left me in the pit of disillusionment. How could God be working this way? Is this the Church I love, where I have found God's love? It challenged me emotionally, intellectually, and religiously. I was changing. Over a period of time, almost like spring supplanting winter, my consternation and confusion began to change. I passed from an intellectual to an emotional conversion to a faith conversion. Growing inside was a deeper and wider and more pervasive trust in the Holy Spirit. If the Spirit could work through so many human obstacles, and the Church continue to preach the good news, and people continue to encounter God in the Church, then indeed the promise of the Lord's Spirit within us was evident. God did not remove our human foibles. God trusts us more than I could imagine. At the edge of losing my faith was a deeper appreciation of salvation and human cooperation. It seemed that it was necessary to lose my presuppositions, intellectual convictions, and emotional preferences in order to find a deeper and purified faith. This experience has continued to be an important parable in my life concerning the unexpected twists and turns of this journey.

While I experienced this conversion in theology, others have similar experiences at worship, in ethical questions, in human relationships. Through each experience, compassion for the human journey with God grows. God and his mysterious ways become more and more central to life: faith in God is the bottom line of every spirituality, especially the theologian's.

Instead of coming up with clear precise answers, theologians open for us a richer diversity of options and the encouragement to follow God in the discipleship to which he calls us.

In decades past, theologians were like homesteaders who had a piece of land, a farm, and fences. Life was clear, chores were constant and regular, life was calm. Theology gave answers. Today, theologians resemble pioneers. They have pulled up stakes, harnessed the wagons, and set off for new and unknown territories. Theology is moving, unsettled, searching for and discovering new territories and peoples. Theology today has more questions than answers, and its answers are less absolute. Moving viewpoints have replaced static ones; the journey has replaced the homestead as metaphor.

Theologians are disciples in the middle of a journey. Because the theologian is a person of faith, of the church, and of the world, the ups and downs of events, people, and him or herself affect the theology. The theologian knows both sides, and the tension between them. Placed as a mediator of the tradition, an interpreter of the past and present, the theologian knows the Church's good points and bad. On the one hand the theologian knows of the Kingdom of God, and on the other hand knows sexism, racism, authoritarianism, and politics in the church. On the one hand the theologian knows that love is the center of human life and on the other hand must allow people to make choices, even fail in their freedom, in order to find God. On the one hand the theologian knows of God's desire for justice, peace, and love in the world, and on the other hand sees poverty, oppression, and violence every day. Theologians do not experience something that others do not. But because of their area of study, their sensitivity is heightened. Theologians are not special; they are specialists. The way the theologian integrates these challenges will most truly reflect the basic presuppositions, direction, and tone of his or her theology.

Theologians immerse themselves in human experience. Sensitized to belief, the theologian will be tested with unbelief. Knowledge is not belief: doctrine is not faith. Begun in Adam and Eve, and continued in all humanity since, and even found in Jesus, the theologian struggles to find the will of God. In so doing, theologians enter into the depths of human unbelief, doubt, and despair. Faith requires it. The theologian cannot draw back from the journey, but must follow Jesus wherever he goes. God's promise in the resurrection is victory over sin and death. The theologian enters these areas armed only with the power of faith, hoping to emerge on the other side victorious in love. The journey is none other than the death-resurrection event of Jesus. Not all are called or chosen to enter into this redemptive action in the same way—but all are called.

Theologians are disciples for all people. Their work might come from a church tradition but it belongs to all people. We journey together as a global community. As learners, disciples help others to come in contact with what it means to be human, and with the Lord who loves us as humans. The word "education" comes from "ex" and "ducere" which mean "to lead out." The action of education is not primarily to put knowledge into a person, but to provide information and skills whereby the person can become whatever he or she wants to be. Theology is no different. Theology offers people the opportunity to develop every dimension of their selves. This requires knowledge.

For example, one's faith might begin in the family, but it grows when other people and events draw it out. One goes to school, meets others, does new activities. Faith changes in relation to these experiences. Just as a mature person does not leave the love of the family, but becomes more a part of it in different ways, so too does one not leave the faith from the family, but matures through different experiences. Knowledge works as a circle: drawing one out and returning one's self in a new way. Whether in a book, a course, a lecture, an article, or a conversation, a theologian offers people a way to see their lives.

Exposure to the word of God in Scripture often opens people to new understandings and horizons. Informing people about the meaning of Jesus, the community called Church, the sacraments, and morality provides true freedom. People's test for validity is often the "correct fit" that these explanations have with their faith experience and with what they already know to be true. A validation of truth takes place. This sounds like intuition but is not; it is knowledge of the heart as opposed to knowledge of the head. It is like two people who love one another and know the truth of that love. Through the same Holy Spirit, the Christian experience of the Lord seems to recognize itself. Hence a major part of a theologian's task is to articulate that experience well. Instead of operating as a cut-and-dried conclusion to a syllogism, theology is persuasive. But this is not enough. We all have intellectual and emotional blockages that resist faith. A conversion process is always required, even of theologians.

Theologians have no special channel to God, no special certainties, and no final solutions. They know that knowledge is not faith, nor can it produce faith. But they also know knowledge can *nourish* faith. One can know how and why one leans with all one's weight, and who the real person is upon whom they lean.

Theologians are people who love the Church. They love both individuals and the corporate person. Theologians love the people of the Philippines or Ghana, even before meeting them. They love those who are dying, and those who are being born. Just as one loves one's country, one's community, one's tribe, one's people, so too does the theologian love the Church as a corporate person—with all its collective humanity. Unless one loves the Church, one cannot continue to do theology as a ministry. It would then only be a job.

Theologians are ministers. They desire to serve the people of God who ask for this ministry. It requires commitment and responsibility, first to the Lord and then to his people. The ministry functions in many different ways: one studies, writes, lectures, teaches or consults. The theologian acts in different capacities and often is simultaneously a professional teacher, administrator, pastor, bishop, wife or husband. According to the needs of both the Church and the theologian, the way of functioning changes throughout life. Anyone may enter into this field at any time either partially or fully.

The joy, service, and help one can contribute to the journey of others keeps the professional theologian theologizing. To see others find God is reward enough. Being part of this process is a privilege. In the end, theologians know that they remain servants of the Lord. Only God can give God; we simply try to remove every obstacle that hinders this relationship, and promote every contribution that helps it. We want to know if that stranger who comes up behind us and walks with us on our journey is the Lord.

This book has come full circle. It began in experience and

ended in experience. The question "What is theology?" was the point of departure. The building blocks were first laid, then the relationships that make up the content of theology, and finally the tools that a theologian uses. Only in this last chapter did we try to touch the intangible: what is theology to one who does it? After the journey through this book, and reflecting upon the passion involved in theology, if a theologian were asked, "What is theology?", one might not be surprised to hear the answer, "Theology? It is a good and faithful friend."

Suggested Readings

Suggested Readings

Introduction

Introductions to theology differ. The most comprehensive is Richard McBrien *Catholicism* (Study Edition) (Minneapolis: Winston Press, 1981). His approach begins in human experience and moves to God, Jesus, and Church. Our approach has been to move from human anthropology to Jesus, God, and us.

A shorter form is Monika Hellwig *Understanding Catholicism* (New York: Paulist Press, 1981). Her book begins with traditional formulations of faith from the past and asks what meaning these have for Christians today. By contrast, our approach has been to begin in human experience, reflect on theology's content, and return to experience.

Part I: The Context of Theology

For a delightful introduction based on story and the bible, see John Shea *Stories of God: An Unauthorized Biography* (Chicago: Thomas More Press, 1978).

For an introduction into the process of theologizing, see J.J. Mueller *What Are They Saying About Theological Method?* (New York: Paulist Press, 1984).

Theological anthropology eventually leads to reading Karl Rahner. One might begin with various popularizations of Rahner and then read his *Foundations of Christian Faith: An Introduction to the Idea of Christianity* (New York: Seabury Press, 1978).

For conversion in Bernard Lonergan, see his *Method in Theology* (New York: Herder and Herder, 1972) and *A Second*

Collection: Papers edited by Wm F.J. Ryan and Bernard J. Tyrrell (London: Darton, Longman and Todd, 1974). For the classic viewpoint from the eyes of liberation theology, see Gustavo Gutierrez *A Theology of Liberation* (Maryknoll, N.Y.: Orbis Books, 1973).

Part II: The Content of Theology

Concerning *Jesus*, many fine works have been written in the last several decades. The list would number in the hundreds. From the viewpoint of doctrine, one might begin with Dermot Lane *The Reality of Jesus* (New York: Paulist Press, 1975) for an overview of Christology. Albert Nolan's *Jesus before Christianity* (Maryknoll, N.Y.: Orbis Books, 1976) is also a good introduction from a South African perspective.

More difficult, Edward Schillebeeckx *Jesus: An Experiment in Christology* (New York: Seabury Press, 1979) and *Christ: The Experience of Jesus as Lord* (New York: Seabury Press, 1980) place Christology in relation to modern scriptural exegesis.

The work of Jon Sobrino *Christology at the Crossroads: A Latin Amercan Approach* (Maryknoll, N.Y.: Orbis Books, 1978) is an important third world view.

Concerning *God*, most systematic theology books include sections on God and are worth consulting. A few would be: John Macquarrie *Principles of Christian Theology* (New York: Scribner, 2nd edition, 1977); Paul Tillich *Systematic Theology* (Chicago: University of Chicago Press, 1951, 1957, 1963. 3 vols); and Karl Rahner. These also present explanations of the trinity.

Concerning *Us*, which includes the church, sacraments, spirituality and prayer, Avery Dulles *Models of the Church* (Garden City, N.Y.: Doubleday and Co., Inc., 1974) is important reading. For Sacraments, a good introduction is Bernard Cooke *Sacraments and Sacramentality* (Mystic, Conn.: Twenty-Third Publications, 1983). The area of spirituality has a plethora of books which have been written in the last decades. One must select an area of interest and proceed accordingly.

Part III: Theology and its Tools

The question of language and texts moves to the area of hermeneutics (interpretation). The major and comprehensive contribution so far is David Tracy's three works *Blessed Rage for Order: The New Pluralism in Theology* (New York: Seabury Press, 1975); *The Analogical Imagination: Christian Theology and the Culture of Pluralism* (New York: Crossroad, 1981); *Plurality and Ambiguity: Hermeneutics, Religion, Hope* (New York: Harper and Row, 1987). Another helpful work is Francis Schussler Fiorenza *Foundational Theology: Jesus and the Church* (New York: Crossroad, 1985). For a general introduction into the problem, see Walter Ong *Orality and literacy: The Technologizing of the Word* (London and New York: Metheun, 1982).